Sabbath as Resilience

Sabbath as Resilience

Spiritual Refreshment for a Stressed-Out World

Edited by
KENNETH J. BARNES
and C. SARA LAWRENCE MINARD

Foreword by Peter S. Heslam

WIPF & STOCK · Eugene, Oregon

SABBATH AS RESILIENCE
Spiritual Refreshment for a Stressed-Out World

Wipf & Stock
An Imprint of Wipf and Stock Publishers
199 W. 8th Ave., Suite 3
Eugene, OR 97401

www.wipfandstock.com

PAPERBACK ISBN: 979-8-3852-3460–8
HARDCOVER ISBN: 979-8-3852-3461-5
EBOOK ISBN: 979-8-3852-3462-2

VERSION NUMBER 032425

To Joanna Mockler, whose vision to establish the Mockler Center for Faith and Ethics in the Public Square at Gordon-Conwell Theological Seminary, and whose ongoing commitment, has inspired countless students, faculty, church leaders, and business community leaders. Her unwavering support of the center has made this book possible.

Contents

Acknowledgements | ix

Foreword | xi
—Peter S. Heslam

Preface | xxix
—Kenneth J. Barnes

Chapter One
The Yoke of Mammon: The Everyday Effects of Economic Stress | 1
—Kenneth J. Barnes

Chapter Two
Prometheus Ascending: From the Atom Bomb to AI | 33
—Kenneth J. Barnes

Chapter Three
Homo Obsessus: Humans Under Siege | 41
—Kenneth J. Barnes

Chapter Four
Sabbath as Resilience | 47
—Kenneth J. Barnes and C. Sara Lawrence Minard

Chapter Five
Sabbath as Reprioritization | 64
—Autumn Alcott Ridenour

—

Chapter Six
Sabbath as Resistance | 79
—Larry O. Natt Gantt, II

Chapter Seven
Sabbath as Reimagination | 99
—Kara Martin

Chapter Eight
Sabbath as Renewal | 115
—C. Sara Lawrence Minard

Chapter Nine
Sabbath as Redemption | 137
—Jeffrey Hanson

Chapter Ten
A View from the Pew | 163
—James F. Longhurst and Kenneth J. Barnes

About the Authors | 179

Acknowledgements

PROJECTS OF THIS NATURE never exist in a vacuum. They happen within the context of our families, our faith communities, our work environments, our academic institutions, and our fields of study. Our ideas are not new; they are built upon the experiences and insights of previous scholars, practitioners, and commentators. This is especially true with a book on Sabbath—a book whose authors are all members of the Mockler Center for Faith and Ethics in the Public Square (Gordon-Conwell Theological Seminary) but who represent very diverse theological, academic, professional, and cultural backgrounds. We must, therefore, take a moment to acknowledge some of the influential people and institutions that have informed and shaped our thinking on the subject.

First, we want to thank Mrs. Joanna Mockler, to whom this book is dedicated, and the fellows and advisors of the Mockler Center, whose work with the center has been invaluable—particularly Dr. Robert Gough (chair of the center's board of advisors) and senior research fellows Dr. Sean McDonough and Dr. Glenn Butner.

Next, we would like to thank our institutions, which have been incubators for this book, especially, Gordon-Conwell Theological Seminary, Harvard University, MIT, Regents Park College (Oxford), Ridley College (Melbourne), Faith in Business (Cambridge), Columbia University, Sciences Po (Paris), High Point University, New College of Florida, and Mary Andrews College College (Sydney). We must also thank those scholars and practitioners who participated in the Redeeming Capitalism Conference at Bretton Woods (2019); their insights provided the inspiration for this book.

We would be remiss not to thank distinguished Professors Abraham Joshua Heschel and Walter Brueggemann whose prolific writings on Sabbath have been instrumental in shaping this discussion.

Of course, a project such as this is only made possible by the professionalism and cooperation of our publisher, Wipf and Stock, and particularly the work of managing editor Matt Wimer and his administrative assistant, George Callihan, our copyeditor, Brittany McComb, and our lead production editor, Ian Creeger. Equally necessary to mention are the indispensable editorial contributions of our family members, such as Debby Barnes, Sarah Gantt, Mick Minard (and no doubt others), and the support of our colleagues, including Janis Flint-Ferguson, Matt Millard, Nicole Olson, and Tom Pfizenmaier, as well as the supportive members of our local congregations.

It is an impossible task to fully acknowledge the many people involved in the development of an idea that ultimately leads to a book. Nor are we able to thank all the people who have nurtured, supported, assisted, encouraged, empowered, and at times even critiqued and corrected us—both throughout our careers and on this project. We therefore ask for an endowment of grace, especially from those whose excellent work on this vast subject we have certainly omitted.

Foreword

PETER S. HESLAM

AT THE TIME OF its opening in 1914, the Panama Canal was the greatest engineering feat in history. With its 51 miles (82 km) of waterway sufficiently deep and wide to allow large shipping vessels to pass between the Atlantic and Pacific Oceans, it transformed global trade. To celebrate its opening, and the human achievement it represented, a universal exhibition (or world's fair) was held in San Francisco from February 20 to December 4, 1915. Known as the Panama-Pacific International Exposition, it was a huge success, attracting around nineteen million visitors. Included among those visitors were the speakers and delegates of the World's Bible Congress, held from August 1 to 4 in one of the exposition's venues.[1]

A keynote speaker at the congress was the eminent American Reformed scholar Benjamin B. Warfield (1851–1921), who at the time was professor of didactic and polemic theology and principal of Princeton Theological Seminary.[2] He was a friend and colleague of the Dutch Reformed theologian, politician, social entrepreneur, university founder, and former prime minister Abraham Kuyper (1837–1920), who had also been invited to speak at the congress. The friendship had been cemented some seventeen years earlier in 1898 when Kuyper, in accepting an invitation for which Warfield was partly responsible, visited Princeton to deliver the prestigious

1. The first world's fair in the United States was the Centennial Exposition in Philadelphia in 1876.

2. Warfield's speech was published as *The Bible: The Book of Mankind*.

xi

Stone Lectures at the seminary and received an honorary doctor-
ate of law from the university.[3] Kuyper had to cancel this second
trip to the USA. Ironically, given the maritime occasion of the
congress, it was due to a shipping hazard. At this juncture in the
Great War (1914–18), transatlantic traffic was at risk from mines
and submarines.[4]

Ever the assiduous publisher, Kuyper ensured that the two
lectures he had prepared for delivery in San Francisco appeared
in print. One of them was titled "The Lord's Day's Observance."[5]
It is clear from this paper that Kuyper's aim was to emphasize the
relevance of biblical teaching on the Sabbath for the whole of life,
rather than simply religious life. He presents the Sabbath as a key
aspect of public theology with universal political and social significance that supersedes and surpasses all religious (and nonreligious) affiliation, tradition, or confession. It is not to be observed,
in the first place, as a religious obligation but as an ordinance built
into creation and inherent in the natural order. "The purpose of my
paper," Kuyper wrote, "is to reprove any un-Evangelical narrow-
ness in the conception of the Lord's day, without loosening a single

3. These lectures, which focused on the historical and contemporary significance of Calvinism, are analyzed in their international context in my *Creating a Christian Worldview: Abraham Kuyper's Lectures on Calvinism*. Kuyper's
invitation was due to the initiative of Geerhardus Vos (1862–1949) but it was
issued on behalf of the faculty of Princeton Theological Seminary, of which
Warfield was a member. A brilliant scholar and linguist, Vos had in 1886 been
invited by Kuyper to become professor of Old Testament at the Free University
of Amsterdam. Still in his early twenties, Vos declined out of deference to his
parents, who had emigrated with him from the Netherlands to the USA only
five years earlier.

4. It has been suggested that Kuyper may also have abandoned his trip
because he did not want to miss making his annual summer visit to a health
clinic near Dresden in Germany. See Kuipers, *Abraham Kuyper*, 477. A revised
and updated version of this comprehensive bibliography is available at The
Neo-Calvinism Research Institute website (https://sources.neocalvinism.org/
kuyper/).

5. Kuyper's other (undelivered) lecture at the World's Bible Congress was
printed as "The Evolution of the Use of the Bible in Europe." Both of these lectures are available in the comprehensive bibliography on The Neo-Calvinism
Research Institute website.

thread of our most serious obligation to observe it." His aim was to trace the fourth commandment back to its "deeper ground" in human nature, thereby showing that "the observance of the Lord's day becomes a problem not exclusively concerning the Church, but a *world problem of universal importance.*"[6]

This book resonates deeply with Kuyper's view. The authors of its chapters also refuse to restrict their focus to the sphere of organized religion but instead explore the ramifications of the Sabbath beyond that sphere. This approach is at least as contrarian today as it was for Kuyper in 1915. For the Sabbath has largely been relegated to a quaint but outdated idea from a bygone age that only has lingering importance to adherents of some religious traditions. But the contrarian purpose and aim of Kuyper's San Francisco paper, cited above, and its congruence with the contents of this book, elicits in this foreword six contrarian (yet biblically grounded) arguments about the Sabbath. The first of these will be Kuyper's argument, examined here in a little more detail.[7]

The Sabbath Is Not Religious

The Sabbath is about the way the world is constituted rather than about a religious code. Kuyper based this argument on the fact that, although the Sabbath is generally associated with the Ten Commandments (where they are enshrined), it actually stems from creation, rather than from religion (Gen 2:2–3). When the Sabbath eventually does appear in religion, in the Ten Commandments as recorded in Exod 20:8–11, there too it is associated with creation. In those verses, the Sabbath's universal significance is reflected not only in their appeal to creation, Kuyper argued, but

---

6. Kuyper, "Lord's Day's Observance," 15 (emphasis original).

7. The rest of this foreword draws on material published in my three-part series of articles in *Faith in Business Quarterly* in 2024 titled "Being Productive: Working from Rest," and on my chapter "The Protestant Rest Ethic: Insights from Abraham Kuyper (1837–1920) on the Sabbath as Good News to the Poor," in *Poverty and the Church* (2025).

in the granting of a weekly day of rest to aliens, and even to slaves and animals (Exod 20:10; cf. Deut 5:14).[8]

Ordinary human experience also reflects that universal significance, Kuyper maintained, as the need for a regular day of rest is evident to everyone, believers and nonbelievers alike.[9] In the wider material world, the Sabbath's universality manifests itself in the rhythms embedded in material existence. As he told his intended audience in San Francisco, the "whole universal system of measures, numbers and moments" is inherent in the rhythmical movement of life: "Life is undulating as a wave undulates, when it is pushed on by the wind."[10] The rhythmical form in poetry reflects, he explains, this wavelike motion. This is suggested by the root of the word "poetry"—ποίησις (*poiesis*)—which in Greek means "creation."[11]

The importance Kuyper attached, in his understanding of the Sabbath, to the idea that one-in-seven is a rhythm built into human and material existence is evidenced in his persistence in conveying it over a period of at least a quarter of a century.[12] But over that time a shift is detectable in the theological framework and language he uses. Whereas in the early phase of his career, he attributed the notion of a one-in-seven day of rest to *natural knowledge*, rather than to specifically *religious knowledge*,[13] as his

8. Kuyper, *Tractaat van den Sabbath*, 136–139, 160, 162.

9. Kuyper, *Our Program*, 83–88. This is an English translation of Kuyper's *Ons Program*, his first major work of political theory and practice.

10. Kuyper, "Lord's Day's Observance," 1. The "system" to which Kuyper refers appears to be all aspects of reality that can be analyzed or observed through the empirical sciences and mathematics.

11. Kuyper, "Lord's Day's Observance," 1. The link Kuyper makes between natural and poetic rhythm finds resonance in the thinking of the poet and essayist T. S. Eliot (1888–1965). In reflecting on the "auditory imagination," Eliot maintained that the human feeling for rhythm penetrates well below conscious levels of thought and feeling. See Eliot, *Use of Poetry and the Use of Criticism*, 119.

12. Kuyper makes this point in his *De Tractaat*, published in 1890, and twenty-five years later in his "The Lord's Day's Observance," published in 1915.

13. See, for instance, *Ons Program*, 231–232 (*Our Program*, 84).

career developed, he articulated this distinction in terms of "common grace" and "special grace".[14]

The urgency with which he considered the issue of rest also increased over time. This is likely to reflect the marked increase during the course of his career in international trade, transport, and communication technology. Roughly three quarters of a century before the contemporary iteration of "globalization" began to take off, and the internet, email, and social media began to proliferate, Kuyper wrote words that seem to anticipate the future:

> But now every perimeter of rest has been dismantled. Electrical wires connect cities and towns to each other, and one country to another. Rail tracks span an entire continent. Mail ships cross all seas. Local markets are no longer anything but subsidiaries, there are no markets at all anymore in this country [the Netherlands] except as auxiliary links, and everything has been drawn together into an all-encompassing global market with which every businessman or tradesman has to deal.
>
> There was a time when mail was delivered at most once per day, but now as many as eight to ten daily deliveries constantly inundate you with new messages and new questions. The telegraph overwhelms you with urgent messages. The telephone distracts your attention from your work. . . . Everything is done in haste without leaving you time to think; you have to grasp quickly what someone is presenting to you and decide immediately.[15]

This culture of hurry and distraction was felt on the Lord's Day: 'Because of the rest it brought to the street, business, and

---

14. Kuyper's massive three-volume treatise on common grace is a compilation of articles published between 1895–1901. All three volumes are available in English translation under the title *Common Grace: God's Gifts for a Fallen World*. For discussions of Kuyper's ideas on common grace, see Heslam, *Creating a Christian Worldview*; and Heslam, "Calvinism in Business—An Enlightened Enterprise?"

15. Kuyper, *Pro Rege*, 1:50–51.

family, the Lord's Day was always the day on which the life of piety came to greatest expression.[16] Now, however:

> On Sundays people want to catch up on what they could not get to during the week, or else they seek respite and relaxation out in nature. Their nerves have been so shaken that they can no longer sit quietly under the preaching of the Word. Rest continues to elude them. There is no place, no time for seclusion. No one even thinks of turning in upon himself anymore. Everything hurries and chases through head and heart. Not even a single moment remains for the soul to be lifted up to God because such a demand is constantly made on the capacities of our thoughts and feelings. Billowing clouds block out the world of the eternal.[17]

Kuyper's thinking about the Sabbath is multifaceted and he expressed it in many publications over his long career. Although an important aspect of them, as revealed in the quote immediately above, was the importance Sunday rest, the scope of his Sabbath thinking was far broader. Indeed, he treated the Sabbath as he treated other biblical and doctrinal themes: as a public theologian, practical politician, and socio-cultural innovator keen to articulate

---

16. Kuyper, *Pro Rege*, 1:48–49.

17. Kuyper, *Pro Rege*, 1:50. In Kuyper's view, the USA, the UK, and the Netherlands had done relatively better than other Western countries at preserving Sunday rest in society at large rather than just among believers. He attributed this in part to the influence of English Reformed theologians (without specifying which ones), whose thinking on this point was embraced by the Dutch Calvinist theologian Gisbertus Voetius (1589–1676). Whereas in the Reformation in the rest of Europe, the significance of the Sabbath was largely restricted to the religious sphere, in the English Reformation its ramifications for wider society were acknowledged. This in turn influenced the USA, as evidenced in the fact that "the whole population was up in arms to enforce the closing of the world's fair in Chicago on Sundays." Kuyper, *Business and Economics*, 94, see also 91–95. The world's fair in Chicago, to which Kuyper refers, took place in 1893, twenty-two years before he was due to address the World's Bible Congress at the world's fair in San Francisco in 1915. The world's fairs continue, albeit they are more commonly referred to as world expositions, or expos (Expo 2030 is due to take place in Riyadh, Saudi Arabia).

and promote their relevance, however contrarian to prevailing norms, to ordinary everyday life.

The Genesis of Rest

We will return to Kuyper, albeit briefly, in the final section before we conclude. But we now turn to the second contrarian proposal about the Sabbath in this foreword. Instead of regarding rest primarily as recovery *from* work, it should be seen as resourcing *for* work. The Bible's first account of creation, told on its opening page, is very brief. Yet what happens each day is broken down into bite-size pieces. Humans are made on the sixth day and are immediately given a job description; they are to be fruitful, subdue the earth, and rule over all that God has made. The reader might expect that the seventh day would depict humans embarking on this work. Instead, no tasks are undertaken, and even God takes a day off. Apparently, therefore, the first day of human existence was a day of rest. Perhaps the only activity humans got up to was walking with God "in the cool of the day" (Gen 2:8).[18]

It is customary in many countries, when chatting with friends and colleagues on Mondays, to ask, "Did you have a good weekend?" It is a fine custom, but it reflects the assumption that the week starts with Monday and ends with Sunday. For centuries, however, Christians have regarded their day of rest—Sunday—as the first day of the week. At its best, it embodied the notion that, given the six days of demanding work that lie ahead, one full day of rest was required. Working from rest is important, in other words, not just resting from work.

We see the principle of working from rest in the life of Jesus. The Gospel writers often show him withdrawing to find solitude before intense periods of ministry (e.g., Mark 1:35). He urges his disciples to do the same on one occasion, before they find themselves involved in a major food hub operation to feed five thousand people (Mark 6:31–32). All this could be the basis for some

18. Unless otherwise indicated, all Scripture quotations in this foreword are taken from the NRSV.

sage advice to "come apart before you fall apart." But on the matter of rest, the Bible goes much further.

The Destiny of Rest

Third, instead of regarding rest merely as an earthly necessity, it should also be regarded as humanity's ultimate destiny. Scripture puts rest at the center of the gospel. In fact, it presents rest as one reason why the gospel is good news. At the very heart of God's offer of salvation in and through Jesus Christ is the offer of rest. That offer, which comes directly from the lips of Jesus, is most elegantly rendered in English as:

> Come unto me, all ye that labour and are heavy laden, and I will give you rest. Take my yoke upon you, and learn of me; for I am meek and lowly in heart: and ye shall find rest unto your souls. For my yoke is easy, and my burden is light. (Matt 11:28–30 AKJV)

More recently, these verses have been imaginatively paraphrased as follows:

> Are you tired? Worn out? Burned out on religion? Come to me. Get away with me and you'll recover your life. I'll show you how to take a real rest. Walk with me and work with me—watch how I do it. Learn the unforced rhythms of grace. I won't lay anything heavy or ill-fitting on you. Keep company with me and you'll learn to live freely and lightly. (MSG)

The idea that rest, rather than redemption, lies at the heart of the gospel may sound almost heretical. It is worth considering, however, the true meaning of redemption. It is a metaphor drawn from the world of finance and it signifies the cancelation of a debt. According to the Hebrew Bible, debts were to be canceled every seven years, during what came to be called the *Shemitah*—the Year of Release or Sabbath Year (Deut 15:1–3). Against this background, the New Testament uses debt as a metaphor for sin against God (Luke 7:41–43; Matt 6:12; 18:21–35; Col 2:13–14).

According to the last of these references, "God forgave us all our sins; he cancelled the unfavourable record of our debts with its binding rules and did away with it completely by nailing it to the cross." Here the apostle Paul is using an additional metaphor to the debt metaphor. As reflected in John's telling of the passion (John 19:16–37), Roman executioners generally nailed to the cross above the head of the condemned person a written statement of their guilt. Paul is saying, accordingly, that our debt records have been included in the destruction and obliteration of the cross. Christ's death cancels debt and thereby inaugurates a perpetual Sabbath year in which the debt of sin is canceled and God's people can enjoy rest—in their earthly lives and beyond (Heb 4). In a very real sense, then, it is for human rest (and the rest of all other parts of the natural world) that Christ died. This means that rest is not "nice to have" for those who can afford luxury holidays and early retirements. Rest lies, instead, at the heart of the gospel and is available to all.

Rest and Productivity

Fourth, instead of perceiving productivity solely as an outcome of work, it should also be perceived as an outcome of rest. This may also sound like dodgy theology. After all, rest is about being unproductive, whereas the Bible seems to recommend productivity. It offers, in fact, the following productivity masterclass: "Go to the ant, you sluggard; consider its ways and be wise! It has no commander, no overseer or ruler, yet it stores its provisions in summer and gathers its food at harvest" (Prov 6:6–8). The apostle Paul may well have taken this masterclass, given his tireless labors (2 Cor 11:21–28) and his injunction that "anyone unwilling to work should not eat" (2 Thess 3:10).

However, the encounter Jesus had with the woman at the well in Samaria helps put the productivity value of hard work into perspective. Here we find Jesus taking a rest: "Jesus, tired as he was from the journey, sat down by the well" (John 4:6). It is a scene not of productivity but of leisure. But nestled in his resting place by the well, Jesus has one of the most amazing conversations in the Gospels. That conversation is all the more amazing for being with a Samaritan (despised by Jews) but also with a woman. Indeed, it is with a woman so disreputable that she needs to draw water from the well at noon, when the need for shelter from the heat was so great she would be less likely to be spotted out in the open.

We have, as a result, one of the most beautiful, vivid, enlightening and convicting passages of Scripture that has helped transform lives around the world, across two millennia. But did the immediate results also reflect such productivity? According to John, the woman responds to Jesus' offer of living water; she then goes to tell her fellow townspeople about Jesus; and then "many Samaritans became believers" (John 4:28, 30, 39–41). The story can function, therefore, as a paradoxical parable about the role of rest in productivity. It provides a model of being productive by working from rest.

It may be objected that productivity is a problematic concept, as it implies that what matters about work is not its intrinsic value but its measurable outcomes. The truth in this view may find support in the fact that the Bible speaks more about fruitfulness than productivity. This begins with the commission given to Adam and Eve, alluded to above, to "be fruitful and multiply" (Gen 1:28). Another way of referring to fruit, however, is "produce." Whatever else a produce stall on a market might sell, it typically includes fruit. Accordingly, the words productivity and fruitfulness are often used interchangeably. However, as the former is the term most often used in the world of business and economics, it is legitimate to use it when seeking to apply to that world what the Bible teaches about fruitfulness. Whether we speak of productivity or of fruitfulness, they both rely on rest.

The Protestant Rest Ethic

Now to this foreword's fifth contrarian proposition. Prevalent in many academic circles is a romantic view of the Middle Ages, in which the Protestant Reformation is perceived as a misguided iconoclasm aimed at destroying some of the best things in human society and culture, including the arts and the associated spheres of entertainment and leisure. It was, as some sociologists have put it, a "desacralization" or "disenchantment" of the sacred. The emphasis on predestination and individual piety left believers feeling uncertain about their salvation. They sought to counteract this uncertainty by creating and accumulating wealth, as wealth was seen as a sign of God's election and favor. The resulting "Protestant work ethic," argued the German sociologist Max Weber (1864–1920), gave rise to capitalism and eventually materialism.[19]

There is no space here to analyze this narrative, sometimes called the "secularization thesis." But the stress in the work of Protestant theologians on the theological importance and contemporary relevance of the notion of Sabbath suggests the need for a more nuanced view. A "rest ethic," it appears, is at least as central to Protestantism as its purported "work ethic." This is reflected, for example, in the work of the leading Protestant theologian and church reformer John Calvin (1509–64). Although he places great value and dignity on human work, he does the same for rest. This is reflected in the extensive attention he gives to the Sabbath in his commentaries and sermons and in his magnum opus, the *Institutes of the Christian Religion*. In fact, in this book he does something surprising for a chief architect of the work ethic: he downplays the command to work in his treatment of the fourth commandment. This commandment reads,

> Remember the Sabbath day, and keep it holy. For six days you shall labour and do all your work. But the seventh day is a Sabbath to the Lord your God; you shall not do any work (Exod 20:8–10a; Deut 5:12–14a).

Whereas Calvin takes resting on the seventh day here as a command, he takes the six days of labor as a "given." Put

19. This "Weber thesis" is famously articulated in Weber's *The Protestant Ethic and the Spirit of Capitalism* (1905). For a discussion of poverty and business in relation to the Weber thesis, see my "Christianity and the Prospects for Development in the Global South," 359–83; "Rise of Religion," 53–72; and "Faith, Fortune and the Future."

grammatically, he takes the verbs in the first sentence of this command as *imperative*, whereas he takes those in the second sentence (without support from the original Hebrew) as merely *indicative*.[20]

In the light of the Weber's thesis, it is perhaps not surprising that Abraham Kuyper, as a Protestant thinker (albeit three and a half centuries after Calvin) also championed the value and dignity of human work. Yet, like Calvin, he dedicates much attention to the Sabbath. His treatise on the Lord's Day, destined for delivery in San Francisco, is but one example of his many writings on this subject.[21] As noted in the case of his San Francisco paper, it is clear from these writings as a whole that his concerns include yet extend far beyond personal spirituality and church practice to encompass the whole of public life and even the whole of material existence. This reflected the fact that Kuyper was not only a public theologian but an active participant in the practical world of politics for almost half a century. It also reflects his emphasis on the all-encompassing scope of the Calvinistic worldview, encapsulated in his most famous quote: "There is not a square inch in the whole domain of our human existence over which Christ, who is sovereign over all, does not call out: 'Mine!'"[22]

Although Protestantism is often held responsible for the desacralization or disenchantment of the sacred, Calvin and Kuyper, as leading representatives of this tradition, can be regarded as providing a sacralization or enchantment of the secular. Their teaching on the Sabbath reflects, in fact, their attempt to dismantle the sacred/secular divide. The Sabbath was not, in Kuyper's words,

20. Calvin, *Institutes*, II.8.28–34.

21. Kuyper, *Lord's Day Observance*. Other key writings by Kuyper on the Sabbath theme include his extensive commentary on the treatment given to the fourth commandment in the compendium of Protestant theology known as the Heidelberg Catechism of 1563, published in English in Kuyper, *On Business and Economics*, 89–122. They also include Kuyper, *Ons Program* (see *Our Program*, 83–88); *Honig uit den Rotssteen*, published in English as *Honey from the Rock*; *Gomer voor den Sabbath*; and *Tractaat*.

22. *On Charity and Justice*, 141. This was said in the address on "sphere-sovereignty" (one of Kuyper's core ideas) that he delivered at the opening of the Free University, which he founded in 1880. A full English translation of this speech can be found in *On Charity and Justice*, 115–49.

about "a spiritual life on one day in the church, and then a spirit-less life for six days in the world."[23] Regarding it as a creational ordinance, rather than merely a religious ordinance, both Calvin and Kuyper treated it as relevant to the whole of "secular" life and as a blessing intended for the whole of humanity. The memory of the day of rest in Eden in the collective consciousness of human-kind had, for Kuyper, kept alive the notion of a day of rest among most people throughout history. Those peoples who had done most to preserve this memory had proved to be the most resilient and courageous.[24] The Sabbath was a gift that allowed people to be spiritually, emotionally, and relationally reequipped to reenter every sphere of life (not just the sphere of organized religion) as transformative agents.

The suggestion that the significance of the Sabbath in the teaching of Reformed theologians amounts to a Protestant "rest ethic" (that complements its "work ethic") may never be widely accepted among scholars. It may also never be generally acknowl-edged that this rest ethic had culture-shaping impact outside the sphere of religion. But the recovery of a theology and praxis of rest is urgent. At a time when global culture is dangerously work obsessed, such a theology and praxis can help address some of the pathologies associated with today's long-hours culture, such as job dissatisfaction, work-related stress, alienation, workaholism, burnout, and all other social ills outlined in this volume.

The Sabbath Is Freedom and Joy

We have arrived at our sixth and final contrarian proposition. De-spite the seriousness of the situation noted at the end of the previ-ous section, very little attention is given to the Sabbath—or even to the general theme of rest—in today's churches. Some of this

23. Kuyper, *On Business and Economics*, 100.

24. Kuyper, *Ons Program*, 231; *Our Program*, 84. The latter English transla-tion of Kuyper's monumental Christian political manifesto renders the Dutch word *veerkrachtig* as "energetic" but "resilient" is more accurate. Clearly Kuyper was an early proponent of "Sabbath as resilience," the theme of this book.

is likely to be linked to the fact that the Ten Commandments, so central to Christian liturgy, theology and ethics for centuries, are rarely given any sustained focus. It is also likely that overly strict and prohibitive observance of the Sabbath in some circles in the past means that the Sabbath is associated with legalism, dullness, and boredom.

But this should not be regarded as inevitable, especially as it is in direct contrast to the celebratory associations the Sabbath has in the Hebrew Bible. It is a day of refreshment (Exod 23:12) and of delight (Isa 58:13), and there is even a "Song for the Sabbath Day" (Ps 92). It is a day not of drudgery but of deliverance—a deliverance so radical and comprehensive that the Sabbath applies (as noted above) to slaves, animals, children, and immigrants (Exod 20:10; Deut 5:14), and can even function as a symbol of so mighty a deliverance as the Exodus (Deut 5:15).

All this is reflected in Jesus' healings on the Sabbath, most especially his healing of a woman with a spirit that had crippled her for eighteen years. When challenged by the synagogue ruler, who is indignant about Jesus healing on the Sabbath, Jesus speaks the language of deliverance: "Ought not this woman, a daughter of Abraham whom Satan bound for eighteen long years, be set free from this bondage on the Sabbath day?" (Luke 13:16). The immediate response of the crowd on that Sabbath day reflects the exuberant celebration of freedom with which the Sabbath was associated: "The entire crowd was rejoicing at [or *were delighted with*] all the wonderful things that he was doing" (Luke 13:17).

Refreshment, delight, freedom, healing, deliverance, exuberance, singing, and rejoicing: What is there not to like about the Sabbath, properly understood? No wonder Jesus said that "the Sabbath was made for humankind, and not humankind for the Sabbath" (Mark 2:27). These words still serve as a challenge, both to those who insist on the strict observance of the Sabbath and to those who regard the Sabbath as a quaint but obsolete stipulation.

Uttered amid the Pharisees' allegations that he and his disciples were breaking the Sabbath by foraging for food, Jesus' words here may appear to downplay the importance of the Sabbath. But the first half of Jesus' sentence—that the Sabbath was made for humankind—requires careful consideration. The background for it is the grinding 24/7 culture in which the Israelites were enslaved in Egypt. Jesus would have been familiar with the Torah's teaching (Deut 5:12–15, as noted above) that keeping the Sabbath was to be a reminder of—and an antidote to—that culture. Far from suggesting that the Sabbath is something from which humans need to be liberated, he is suggesting that it liberates. It is intended to set them free to experience God's shalom.

Contemporary culture is in danger of returning to the bondage culture of ancient Egypt. Making bricks without straw to preserve the wealth and power of a tiny elite is the experience of many workers today. Even in highly paid work, the blurring of boundaries between labor and leisure, made possible by improvements in electronic communication, is producing a generation of spiritual, emotional, and relational captives. It is perhaps not surprising that we are facing such high levels of burnout and a mental health crisis. Sabbath is neither an unbending rule nor a useless remnant from another age. It is a pathway to blessing and one of God's richest gifts to human beings.

This foreword is intended merely to pique the interest of those who plan to read the contributions that follow. It does so by making six proposals about the Sabbath that may be contrarian but are also intensely positive and uplifting. They are that the Sabbath is not religious but universal; it is not only about resting from work but about working from rest; it is not merely a temporary necessity but an eternal destiny; it is not a drag but a spur to productivity; it has inspired not only a work ethic but a rest ethic (the latter, urgently in need of recovering today); it is not about legalism, dullness, and boredom but about freedom, delight, and joy.

In the midst of a culture of stress, distraction, and overwork, it is time to heed the call of this book for the rediscovery of the Sabbath as resilience, reprioritization, resistance, reimagination, and redemption. That call can also inspire further thinking about some other important Sabbath-related rediscoveries we need to make, some of which also happen to begin with the letter *R*: rest, retreat, review, reflection, renewal, and recreation. For the Sabbath is full of resources, riches, and rewards. It is a precious gift from God. That gift, freely available in this life, can deliver humans from the oppressive culture of overwork they have created. And it is offered to them as their eternal treasure in the life to come. This book offers a key to unlocking that potential.

Bibliography

Calvin, John. *Institutes of the Christian Religion*. Vol. 1. Edited by Ford Lewis Battle and John T. McNeill. Louisville, Kentucky: 1960.

Eliot, T. S. *The Use of Poetry and the Use of Criticism: Studies in the Relation of Criticism to Poetry in England*. London: Faber & Faber, 1933.

Heslam, Peter S. "Being Productive: Working from Rest." (Part 1) *Faith in Business Quarterly* 22.4 (Nov. 2023) 36.

———. "Being Productive: Working from Rest." (Part 2) (Part 2)*Faith in Business Quarterly* 23.1 (Apr. 2024) 36.

———. "Being Productive: Working from Rest." (Part 3) *Faith in Business Quarterly* 23.2 (Aug. 2024) 35–36.

———. "Calvinism in Business—An Enlightened Enterprise?: Abraham Kuyper, Common Grace, and the Potential of Business." Introduction to *On Business and Economics* by Abraham Kuyper, xix–xl. Edited by Peter S. Heslam. Bellingham, WA: Lexham / Action Institute, 2021.

———. "Christianity and the Prospects for Development in the Global South." In *The Oxford Handbook of Christianity and Economics*, edited by Paul Oslington, 359–83. Oxford: Oxford University Press, 2014.

———. *Creating a Christian Worldview: Abraham Kuyper's Lectures on Calvinism*. Grand Rapids/Cambridge, UK: Eerdmans, 1998.

———. "Faith, Fortune and the Future: Christianity and Enterprise in Human Development." *Religions* 12 (2021) 1039. https://doi.org/10.3390/rel12121039.

———. "The Protestant Rest Ethic: Insights from Abraham Kuyper (1837–1920) on the Sabbath as Good News to the Poor." In *Poverty and the Church*, edited by Muthuraj Swamy and Philip Powell. Cambridge, UK: Cambridge Centre for Christianity Worldwide, 2025.

———. "The Rise of Religion and the Future of Capitalism." In *De Ethica* 2.3 (2015) 53–72

Kuipers, Tjitze. *Abraham Kuyper: An Annotated Bibliography 1857–2010*. Boston: Brill, 2011.

Kuyper, Abraham. *Common Grace: God's Gifts for a Fallen World*. 3 vols. Bellingham, WA: Lexham, 2015–2020.

———. *The Evolution of the Bible in Europe.* Gravenhage, NL: Bootsma, 1915.

———. *Gomer voor den Sabbath: Meditatiën over en voor den Sabbath.* Amsterdam: Wormser, 1889.

———. *Honey from the Rock: Daily Devotions from Young Kuyper.* Bellingham: Lexham, 2018.

———. *Honig uit den Rotssteen.* 2 vols. Amsterdam: Kruyt, 1880–83.

———. "The Lord's Day's Observance." The Hague: Js. Bootsma, 1915. https://www.delpher.nl/nl/boeken/view?coll=boeken&identifier=MMKB21:041130000:00001.

———. *Pro Rege: Living Under Christ's Kingship.* 3 vols. Bellingham: Lexham, 2016–19.

———. *On Business and Economics.* Edited by Peter S. Heslam. Bellingham, WA: Lexham / Action Institute, 2021.

———. *On Charity and Justice.* Edited by Matthew J. Tuininga. Bellingham: Lexham, 2022.

———. *Ons Program.* Amsterdam: Kruyt, 1879.

———. *Our Program: A Christian Political Manifesto.* Bellingham, WA: Lexham, 2015.

———. *Tractaat van den Sabbath: Historische dogmatische studie.* Amsterdam: Wormser, 1890.

Warfield, Benjamin, B. "The Bible: The Book of Mankind". *A paper delivered at the World Bible Conference* (San Francisco, CA, Aug. 1-4, 1915). New York: American Bible Society, 1915.

Weber, Max. *The Protestant Ethic and the Spirit of Capitalism.* London: George Allen & Unwin, 1930.

Preface

KENNETH J. BARNES

AS OF THIS WRITING, there is a lot for people to feel stressed about. War is rife, with major conflicts in the Middle East and Eastern Europe dominating the headlines.[1] Consumer inflation is making it ever more difficult for families to make ends meet,[2] and higher interest rates are negatively impacting the housing market while simultaneously driving up rents.[3] Nearly two-thirds (65 percent) of all Americans are living "paycheck to paycheck,"[4] and personal debt is at an all-time high.[5]

The political climate is disturbingly toxic, with extreme views being amplified by social media and exploited by political opportunists.[6] Racial tensions and xenophobia are at levels not seen since the 1960s, and both anti-Semitism and Islamophobia are on the rise.[7]

Despite its amazing benefits, information technology has revealed its "dark side," as our mobile devices appear to enslave us; algorithms prey upon us; and concerns over the misuse of artificial intelligence conjure up visions of a dystopian future where

1. Economist, "From Gaza to Ukraine."
2. Fernando, "What Is the Consumer Price Index?"
3. Herbert, "Home Prices."
4. Leonhardt, "Living Paycheck to Paycheck."
5. Federal Reserve Bank of New York, "Household Debt."
6. Mamakos and Finkel, "Social Media Discourse."
7. Yank, "Islamophobia and Antisemitism."

machines displace people and the human mind becomes an obsolete artifact of a bygone era.[8]

For the first time in generations, life-expectancy in the United States is in decline.[9] Meanwhile, annual healthcare costs in the United States have risen to 4.5 trillion dollars (17.3 percent of GDP),[10] with medical debt cited as a leading cause of personal bankruptcy.[11] Gun deaths continue to climb toward fifty thousand per year, over half of which are suicides.[12] After years of improvement, divorce figures ticked upward during the pandemic,[13] and reports of anxiety and/or depressive disorders (especially among young adults) also rose;[14] and the American Psychiatric Association has declared excess stress a "national mental health crisis."[15]

Additionally, the COVID-19 pandemic left behind a complex legacy of despair and distrust—despair over the human toll of the disease itself and distrust of those who sought to mitigate its effects. Lockdowns brought disruption to every aspect of society, from classrooms to supply chains, from church services to family reunions. What some saw as governments exercising their rightful duty to "preserve, protect and defend," others saw as the "Deep State" overstepping its bounds and exerting undue influence over the lives of individuals. Novel treatments, designed to stop the spread of the disease were greeted with widespread skepticism; and interventions designed to keep the economy going were met with derision.[16] Fissures in the body politic were further exacerbated in the aftermath of the 2020 presidential election, when, on January 6, 2021, amidst unproven accusations of voter fraud, an

---

8. Cleveland Clinic, "Technophobia."

9. Harvard T.H. Chan School of Public Health, "Life Expectancy Decline."

10. Centers for Medicare and Medicaid Services, "Health Expenditure Data."

11. Braydon, "States Confront Medical Debt."

12. Gramlich, "Data About Gun Deaths."

13. Bieber, "Divorce Statistics in 2024."

14. American Psychiatric Association, "What Are Anxiety Disorders?"

15. Evans et al., "Stress in America."

16. Priniski and Holyoak, "Darkening Spring."

angry mob failed in its attempt to thwart the peaceful transfer of power through violent means.

Finally, the church in America is in serious decline, with church attendance still below pre-pandemic levels,[17] and many Christians feeling marginalized, at best, and persecuted, at worst.[18]

It is no wonder that people feel anxious and angry, hopeless and disillusioned, misunderstood and under attack. They are seeking accessible solutions to complicated situations, or at the very least, mechanisms to help them cope with the debilitating effects of extreme stress and pervasive uncertainty. They are in desperate need of resilience but are ill equipped to find it.[19]

It is against this backdrop that the fellows of the Mockler Center for Faith and Ethics in the Public Square (Gordon-Conwell Theological Seminary) met to consider what tools the church and the academy have at their disposal to help combat the current crisis and its accompanying malaise. During the pandemic, the center began hosting a series of live stream events under the banner "Fear, Facts and Faith," where experts and thought leaders in their respective fields, engaged with theologians, pastors, and the public to dispel misinformation and explore what the Bible and the church have to say about complex social issues, including their causes, their effects, and how we may address them.[20]

As it turns out, they not only have much to say, but they also offer many remedies, including one particular antidote that harkens back to the very beginning of the biblical metanarrative—namely, the gift of Sabbath. Before exploring the phenomenon of Sabbath more closely, however, we would do well to unpack the nature of the malady more deeply, especially some of the economic, the technological, and the cultural ills that impact us all.

17. Jones, "U.S. Church Attendance."

18. Yancey, "Is There Discrimination?"

19. Zimmerman, "What Makes People Resilient?"

20. See the series web page "Fear, Facts and Faith" at https://www.gordon-conwell.edu/fear-facts-faith/.

Bibliography

American Psychiatric Association. "What Are Anxiety Disorders?" Last updated June 2023. https://www.psychiatry.org/patients-families/anxiety-disorders/what-are-anxiety-disorders.

Bieber, Christy. "Revealing Divorce Statistics in 2024." *Forbes*, Nov. 20, 2024. https://www.forbes.com/advisor/legal/divorce/divorce-statistics/.

Braydon, Jesse. "States Confront Medical Debt That's Bankrupting Millions." AP News, Apr. 12, 2023. https://apnews.com/article/medical-debt-legislat ion2a4f2fab7e2c58a68ac4541b8309c7aa.

Centers for Medicare and Medicaid Services. "National Health Expenditure Data." Last updated Sept. 10, 2024. https://www.cms.gov/data-research/statistics-trends-and-reports/national-health-expenditure-data.

Cleveland Clinic. "Technophobia." Last updated Apr. 20, 2022. https://my.clevelandclinic.org/health/diseases/22853-technophobia.

Economist. "From Gaza to Ukraine, Wars and Crises Are Piling Up." Nov. 18, 2023. https://www.economist.com/international/2023/11/13/from-gaza-to-ukraine-wars and crises-are-piling-up.

Evans, Arthur C., et al. "Stress in America 2020: A National Mental Health Crisis." American Psychological Association. Oct. 2020. https://www.apa.org/news/press/releases/stress/2020/sia-mental health-crisis.pdf.

Federal Reserve Bank of New York. "Household Debt and Credit Report (Q3 2023)." 2024. https://www.newyorkfed.org/microeconomics/hhdc.

Fernando, Jason. "What is the Consumer Price Index (CPI)?" *Investopedia*, October 24, 2024. https://www.investopedia.com/terms/c/consumerpriceindex.asp.

Gramlich, John. "What the Data Says About Gun Deaths in the U.S." Pew Research Center. April 26, 2023. https://www.pewresearch.org/short-reads/2023/04/26/what-the-data-says-about-gun-deaths-in-the-u-s/.

Harvard T.H. Chan School of Public Health. "What's Behind 'Shocking' U.S. Life Expectancy Decline." Last updated Nov. 22, 2024. https://hsph.harvard.edu/news/whats-behind-shocking-u-s-life-expectancy-decline-and-what-to-do-about-it/.

Herbert, Chris. "Home Prices and Rents Remain High, as Steep Interest Rates Lock Homeowners In Place and Slow Construction." Joint Center for Housing Studies of Harvard University. June 21, 2023. https://www.jchs.harvard.edu/blog/home-prices-and-rents-remain-high-steep-interest-rates-lock-homeowners-place-and-slow.

Jones, Jeffrey M. "U.S. Church Attendance Still Lower Than Pre-Pandemic." Gallup. June 26, 2023. https://news.gallup.com/poll/507692/church-attendance-lower-prepandemic.aspx.

Leonhardt, Megan. "Living Paycheck to Paycheck Is Common, Even Among Those Who Make More Than $100,000." Barron's. Last updated Oct. 15, 2023. https://www.barrons.com/articles/living-paycheck-consumer-economy-bb16b8e8.

Mamakos, M. and Finkel, E. "The Social Media Discourse of Engaged Partisans Is Toxic Even When Politics Are Irrelevant." Institute for Policy Research, Northwestern University (October 2023). https://doi.org/10.1093/pnasnexus/pgad325.

Priniski, J. Hunter, and Keith J. Holyoak. "A Darkening Spring: How Preexisting Distrust Shaped COVID-19 Skepticism." *PLOS One* 17.1 (2022). https://pmc.ncbi.nlm.nih.gov/articles/PMC8791533/.

Yancey, George. "Is There Really Anti-Christian Discrimination in America?" Gospel Coalition. Aug. 19, 2019. https://www.thegospelcoalition.org/article/anti-christian-discrimination-america/.

Yank, Maya. "Islamophobia and Antisemitism on the rise in US amid Israel-Hamas War." *Guardian*, Nov. 10, 2023. https://www.theguardian.com/us-news/2023/nov/10/us-islamophobia-antisemitism hate-speech-israel-hamas-war-gaza.

Zimmerman, Eilene. "What Makes Some People More Resilient Than Others?" *New York Times*, last updated June E, 2020. https://www.nytimes.com/2020/06/18/health/resilience-relationships-trauma.html.

Chapter One

The Yoke of Mammon
The Everyday Effects of Economic Stress

Kenneth J. Barnes

The word mammon (ΜΑΜΩΝᾷ) appears only four times in the New Testament (Matt 6:24; Luke 16:9, 11, 13). In each instance it is used by Jesus to describe material wealth. It is probably derived from *mamona* (אָנוֹמְמָ) in Aramaic (the *lingua franca* of many Palestinian Jews in the first century CE), meaning a "treasure in which one puts their trust." In Matthew, it is found in the Sermon on the Mount (Matt 6:24) and in Luke, the so-called parable of the dishonest steward (Luke 16:9–11). In contrast to the more common word for treasure (θησαυρός) found throughout the New Testament, its juxtaposition with God (θεός), who is to be served (δουλεύω), in the Matthew passage suggests that mammon possesses some agency, capable of tempting one away from God. This led to the church's general personification of mammon as early as

1

the fourth century CE and the specific identification of mammon as an evil deity in the Middle Ages.[1]

The personification of mammon need not be taken literally for the image to ring true. While mammon itself may be a metaphor for the negative impact of both individual bad actors and malignant systems, the effects are the same. People feel oppressed by forces they cannot see and appear beyond their control; they are hurting and they're looking for ways to cope.

In the autumn of 2019 (prior to the aforementioned "Fear, Facts and Faith" series), the Mockler Center convened a distinguished group of Christian leaders from the church, the academy and the marketplace to explore the conditions that contribute to economic and workplace stress. The group included CEOs and those whose ministries (both church and parachurch) serve business leaders as well as economists from secular universities and theological scholars. They came from diverse backgrounds, political affiliations, and faith traditions; each came with a wealth of knowledge and experience; and all came with a genuine desire to better understand the difficult challenges faced by people of faith at work and in business. Following are some of the more common issues shared by the delegates, revealing how and why people feel overwhelmed by their circumstances and subjugated by a vast, powerful, and impersonal economic ecosystem.

Embedded Systems

First among the challenges mentioned by delegates were the "embedded systems" that drive so much of our economic behavior. Some of these systems are internal and unique to particular organizations, while others are endemic to entire sectors.

One feature of these embedded systems is an inherent resistance to change (RTC), both individually and corporately, that makes it very difficult for conscientious actors to improve working conditions. As Rehman et al. note, despite decades of research

---

1. Pope, "Mammon," para. 1.

and the introduction of countless change management programs across institutions large and small, the overwhelming majority of change management efforts fail.[2] Most of those failed efforts have only to do with business processes or organizational changes, not the more difficult task of changing employee behavior and/or informing corporate cultural. Despite the desire of people of faith to effect transformation in both the workplace and the economy as a whole, resistance to change persists.[3]

As the research demonstrates, there are good reasons behind RTC.[4] Many change agents are insensitive to the fear and disruption caused by their actions, and many fail to acknowledge the costs associated with change. The result is a tendency for individuals and organizations to resist change, and if permitted, revert to familiar ways, even if it means suffering the consequences of failing to adapt to medium and long-term threats.

This phenomenon is not restricted to individual organizations but is evident across entire sectors. Take for example, the author's own sector of theological higher education. Prior to 1999, the Association of Theological Schools didn't permit any online courses at its accredited institutions and no fully online degrees were permitted until 2013.[5] Despite the association's recognition of the need for more online degrees, prior to the COVID-19 pandemic, only a fraction of the association's accredited institutions offered them, with the larger, well-established, residential seminaries leading the resistance. Since the pandemic however, and the normalization of online teaching, the entire higher education sector is dealing with the effects of RTC, with those institutions less resistant to change reaping the benefits of market disruption[6] and those organizations that continue to resist, experiencing steep declines in enrollment and fiscal trauma. This has resulted in increased stress across the entire higher education spectrum,

2. Rehman, "Psychology of Resistance," paras. 1–5.
3. Folger and Konovsky, *Effects*, 115–30.
4. Ford, *Resistance to Change*, 362–77.
5. Tanner, "Online Learning," 1–3.
6. Shankar, *Evidence*, 242–49.

3

increasing the experience of burnout and decreasing levels of levels of satisfaction, among faculty (especially junior, nontenured faculty) and administrators alike.[7] It is a system-wide problem, but individuals are suffering from its effects.

This of course is not unique to higher education; other well attested examples include disruptions in retail, entertainment, travel and tourism, banking and finance, computing, automotive, and countless other sectors. In fact, RTC has put many well-known companies (including highly recognized brands) out of business, while those that have adapted to change often did so at great expense to their organizations and considerable pain to their employees. Overcoming RTC is a very difficult task, but research has shown that it can be done if people believe that there is a just (a.k.a., virtuous) cause behind the change.[8] Perceived economic efficiency alone, however, is an insufficient motive for people to change their behavior. There must be more at stake than a performance review for people to disrupt the status quo.

Another challenge cited by the delegates, one which falls under the categories of both embedded systems and RTC, is the impact of entrenched power structures, both internally and externally. As Rodrigues et al. and others have noted, the power of top-line managers to enhance their own power bases through a constellation of asymmetric information, consolidated relationships, and control over resources, helps to create environments that are resistant to change.[9] In fact, those who propose change are often targeted by top-line managers as threats to their hegemony and are often subjected to "neutralization" efforts.

Similarly, rigid reporting structures can also be detrimental to the work of change agents themselves, if the proposed changes are seen as threats to the autonomy of superiors. In the case of one delegate to the conference, his entire career had once been jeopardized by failing to respect an unofficial chain of command protocol within his company. Noticing that morale was down and that

7. Xu and Wang, "Job Stress," paras. 1–33.
8. Rehman, "Psychology of Resistance," paras. 1–5.
9. Rodrigues and António, "Managers' Entrenchment," 39–50.

many of the company's employees were people of faith, he raised the prospect of a corporate chaplaincy program to the company's CEO. The proposed chaplaincy had little to do with the employee's work responsibilities or the responsibilities of his supervisor. It was simply a helpful suggestion, designed to supplement the company's existing employee assistance program (EAP), and was ultimately a matter for the department of human resources and the company's executive committee. The reporting protocols of the company were so stringent however that despite the CEO's interest in the project, the employee's immediate supervisor vetoed the suggestion in response to what he saw as the employee's impertinence in "going over his head." The employee was devastated, and the company never enjoyed the potential benefits of the program.

This example is not unique to one person's experience. It is quite common for change agents to experience the wrath of both peers and supervisors, as attested to by several conference participants.

Another inhibitor to change that might be considered the result of "embedded systems," is the increasing constraint on employees' time, as staffing shortages, increased workloads, and employer expectations make it difficult for employees to think about anything other than the immediate task at hand. For many, gone are the days when employees were encouraged, and even empowered, to think about ways to improve processes and increase customer satisfaction, as speed, growth, innovation, agility, and cost reductions have become the primary focus of many businesses today.[10] If employees don't have the time to think creatively about how to improve their own businesses, how can they possibly attempt to transform the way people think about the impact of their actions on both the general economy and on society as a whole? The answer is, they can't—unless they are willing to go against the grain and risk the probable repercussions.

Many will remember, in the aftermath of energy giant Enron's demise, hearing on the news recordings of Enron's traders manipulating energy prices in order to increase the company's profits,

10. Edwards, "Whatever Happened," paras. 1–9.

even though their manipulation caused tremendous pain and suffering among unsuspecting consumers.[11] When one trader was heard on the recordings questioning the ethics of their actions, he was immediately silenced by a fellow trader, who appealed to both the vagaries of "market forces" and the necessity of immediate action to secure the highest possible price for the company. The conscientious objector was overruled by his peers and the company profited accordingly, at least in the short term. In the long run, however, Enron's corrupt culture ultimately led to its demise and thousands of innocent people paid dearly for Enron's turpitude.

This of course, brings us to another element of embedded systems as an impediment to meaningful change, and that is the area of assessment metrics. The old adage that people will do what they are incentivized to do is as true today as ever. Sadly, the metrics against which most employees are measured today tend to be very narrowly focused, financial results. This is true of individuals and corporations alike, with individual employees' compensation often pegged to departmental, divisional, or company financial goals and executive compensation tied to company profits or, more likely, publicly traded share prices.

While the Enron bankruptcy, the collapse of Lehman Brothers, the Libor scandal, the Madoff pyramid scheme, the collapse of FTX, and countless other examples of corporate malfeasance are proof positive of the need for systemic change, they are also examples of what happens when performance metrics are reduced to nothing more than short-term monetary results. The fact that most companies are in the business of generating profits and returns for their shareholders is obvious. Unfortunately, as noted by the author in a previous work and others,[12] the outsized influence of this brute fact often leads to a combination of short-termism, greed, unethical behavior, unlawful practices, and catastrophic business failures and must be challenged as the *solus finus* of business. Until it is challenged however, most people will simply follow

---

11. Nix, "Enron," 765–802.

12. See Barnes, *Redeeming Capitalism*.

the crowd, without realizing the long-term damage they are doing to themselves and others.

Lack of Control

The next most commonly mentioned inhibitor to effecting meaningful change and transforming economic behavior is what symposium delegates simply described as "lack of control." That is not to say that change agents don't have the ability to influence behavior and culture; it simply means that external influences will often dictate the *foci* of organizations' attention to the point where control over narratives, events, policies, procedures, and the use of scarce resources are concentrated among too few actors.

First among those external influences is the market itself. Every business (and it may be argued every organization) is subject to the vagaries of ever-changing markets. In theology and philosophy, we speak of the "marketplace of ideas," where new concepts constantly challenge old assumptions, which require appropriate responses. In business and economics, however, markets are driven simply by supply and demand, and changes in demand, brought about by new market entrants, new technologies, or other factors can put tremendous strain on companies' assets (especially cash), and force businesses into survival mode. When businesses and organizations find themselves facing existential threats, it is not uncommon for more lofty ambitions to be relegated to the dustbin of relative obscurity.

This is especially true of publicly traded companies, where the pressure to "outperform the market" is relentless. Shareholders vote with their money; underperforming stocks may be dropped in a nanosecond and executives replaced at the whim of their boards. This pressure makes it very difficult, even for senior executives, to influence corporate behavior in ethically positive ways if it is determined that ethical behavior comes at a financial cost.

The experience of one of the conference delegates is a stark reminder of this reality. The delegate in question was a senior executive at a multibillion-dollar company, responsible for one of the corporation's international businesses. As with most companies of its size, they operated via a "matrix" organizational structure. Business units operate "vertically" and have profit and loss (P&L) responsibility for their divisions, while headquarters-based executives operate "horizontally" and are responsible for business processes and policies. When there is a dispute between executives as to the effects of a particular business decision and/or policy, it is not uncommon for the most senior executives (including the CEO) to arbitrate between the opposing sides.

In the case of the delegate's situation, a disagreement arose over how to deal with a labor dispute at one of the company's international factories. The company had decided to close one of their manufacturing sites and relocate it elsewhere (in the same country) for sound business reasons. However, local law allowed workers to protest the closure and force the company to "show cause" to the satisfaction of the local government. This could be a time-consuming process and would probably mean a delay in the transfer of their operations to the new location, costing the company a considerable amount of money.

The executives at headquarters wanted to respond to the situation by withholding the wages of the petitioning workers in the hope that, by "squeezing them," they would withdraw their complaint and the factory relocation (which was inevitable) would take place according to the company's timetable. The delegate however (who was responsible for the business's P&L) believed that to be grossly unethical and potentially illegal. He believed it better to "do the right thing" and suffer the financial consequences than to break the law and/or create ill will among the employees, some of whom would be moving to the new facility and continuing to work for the company. He made his case as eloquently and forcefully as possible but was sadly overruled by the headquarters-based executives. He simply didn't have enough control over the situation (despite his elevated status) to transform the thinking of his most senior colleagues.

As one considers the particulars of this scenario, it soon becomes clear that the problem wasn't a bad policy or even a disagreement between executives; the problem was the culture of the company—a culture where the "maximization of shareholder value" trumped all other considerations. Even though both the company's mission statement and its values statement begin with a commitment to "high ethical standards," the company continues to put profits before people (or anything else). It should therefore come as no surprise to learn that the company in question has recently been cited by various regulators for hundreds of employment and environmental violations. Ironically, those violations have resulted in the company having to pay millions of dollars in fines, calling into question the economic wisdom of unethical behavior to begin with.

Corporate Culture

Corporate cultures, like all cultures, evolve over time. They are a constellation of many and varied influences and experiences and are difficult to inform and even more difficult to change. In a rudimentary sense, however, the basic building blocks of most cultures are shared values, shared language, and shared experiences. For example, more than the food or the wine or the fashion, French culture is built upon its values (*liberté, égalité, fraternité*), its language (which is legally protected by the *Académie française*) and two-thousand years of Gallic history. The same may be said of countless other countries, and the model holds true for most organizations and businesses as well.

When cultures get into trouble, however, it is often because of a misalignment between an entity's aspirational values and its praxis. This is often noted, for example, by social commentators, critical of America's failure to live up to the values articulated in its foundational documents. To state that the "equality" of persons is a "self-evident truth"[13] while denying basic rights and freedoms to large swathes of the population creates an unresolved tension that often leads to social discord, distrust, and cynicism. The same

13. Jefferson et al., "Declaration of Independence."

may be said of many companies today, leading to the corruption of many corporate cultures. Corrupt corporate cultures produce many unwanted and unintended consequences, which make effecting positive change extremely difficult.

Among those unwanted and unintended consequences is the fostering of toxic work environments. A recent MIT study[14] on the causes of the so-called "great resignation" (discussed further below) indicates that the presence of a toxic work environment is by far the leading indicator of why a person would choose to leave their place of employment. One of the elements of a toxic work environment is a workplace where unethical behavior is normalized. Logic would have it that an organization that forces out people of conscience will be populated by a higher percentage of people who condone, or at least tolerate, unethical behavior. That makes it much more difficult for people of faith, and/or any people of good will, to effect transformational change.

Similarly, businesses and organizations with a low level of trust between management and frontline workers, and among frontline workers themselves, are likely to have corporate cultures that are resistant to positive change. Workplace consultant and best-selling author Stephen M. R. Covey, in his book *Trust and Inspire*, cites countless examples of organizations that have failed to react to the realities of the post-pandemic world, largely due to low-trust / slow-to-change cultures. Conversely, those organizations where trust is high have a much better track record of effecting change.[15]

This was the experience of conference delegates as well. Many reported the dangers of challenging unethical behavior, questioning the decisions of superiors, or taking a minority position on moral grounds. Sometimes derided for their religious beliefs, delegates could find themselves in situations where taking a moral stand was viewed as proselytization, even when their complaints were in keeping with the company's policies. In the case of one delegate, he had been accused of "imposing" his religious beliefs

14. Sull et al., "Toxic Culture."
15. Covey, *Trust.*

on his fellow employees because he came to the defense of a female employee whom others were speaking of in a sexually explicit manner. The company's harassment policies forbade such conduct, yet he became the object of ridicule for being a "prude." Such encounters destroy trust in an organization and dramatically increase the risks associated with ethical advocacy.

Closely related to a general lack of trust in an organization is a culture built upon the exploitation of employees, who are no longer viewed as people but as easily replaceable commodities. Ironically, recent research has shown that companies who treat their employees as dispensable increase their rates of attrition.[16] Corporate cultures suffer when turnover is high, as the cost of attrition and the lack of meaningful relationships create work environments that are simply less desirable and therefore less productive.[17]

Lastly, the effects of workplace stress and widespread burnout are two other factors that contribute to corporate cultures that are resistant to meaningful change. Simply put, it takes a lot of energy to be a change agent, and delegates to the conference reported feeling "overworked and under-appreciated." This of course, saps people's energy and disincentivizes them in their efforts to lead the difficult process of renewal and transformation. The complications caused by the COVID-19 pandemic have only made things worse and made the need for change more urgent.

Post-COVID-19 Economic Fault Lines

The economic effects of the COVID-19 pandemic will be felt for years, if not an entire generation. It exposed the fragility of global supply chains and the challenge of mutually interdependent economies. This became evident in the earliest days of the pandemic when shortages in the supply of personal protective equipment (PPE) resulted in a "beggar-thy-neighbor" scramble for gloves,

---

16. Zweig and Zhao, "Greener Pastures," 1–23.
17. Hall, "Cost," paras. 1–20.

masks, shields, and other safety devices.[18] Local and state governments competed for scarce resources on the open market while federal governments commandeered factories and converted them into temporary manufacturers of PPE and ventilators. The disruption to business was immense, but the reality of a deadly disease of unknown origin, with no known treatment, trumped all other considerations.

As governments around the world began to issue isolation orders, lockdowns, and other strict containment measures, the global economy suffered a seismic shock. To "keep the plates spinning," governments and central banks flooded the global economy with cash. As a result, sovereign debt alone rose by twenty-four trillion US dollars[19] during the pandemic, and central banks added another ten trillion US dollars[20] to their balance sheets over the same period. This level of fiscal and monetary intervention was unprecedented, and space here does not permit an apposite critique of its effects. Suffice to say, however, when Russia invaded neighboring Ukraine in early 2022, sending both energy and grain prices soaring, the combination of these phenomena created inflationary pressures that haven't been seen in nearly forty years.[21]

In an effort to bring inflation under control, governments and central banks have since begun to tighten the money supply, raising the specter of a global recession. While at the time of writing no such recession has materialized, businesses large and small are beginning to brace for one, as many have announced significant layoffs in an effort to protect their own balance sheets and "stay ahead of the curve."[22]

In the meantime, individuals and businesses are still coming to terms with both the long-term effects of the aforementioned "great resignation" and the long-term impact of working from home (WFH), which during the pandemic was convenient and

18. Barnes and Hoffmires, "TrueFootprint," 20–29.

19. Jones, "COVID Response," para. 1.

20. Cukierman, "COVID-19," paras. 1–61.

21. Harrison, "How High Is Inflation?," para. 1.

22. Balu, "Amazon," paras. 1–13.

cost effective on one level but both intrusive and disruptive on another.

Research by the Federal Reserve Bank of Dallas suggests that WFH increased from 8.2 percent of the workforce before CO-VID-19 to 35.2 percent of the workforce (a more than 300 percent increase) in the first three months of the pandemic alone.[23] The advantages of this shift are obvious. Workers who were forbidden from congregating at their places of work were still able to carry out many (if not most) of their duties, and companies were able to stay in business. Commuting to work was reduced proportionately saving employees money, while simultaneously reducing CO_2 emissions. Commuting time was also returned to employees, along with the convenience and cost savings of not having to "dress properly" for work. Employees could work from virtually anywhere that had a decent internet connection, with many people leaving large cities in favor of less crowded, less expensive towns and villages.

However, there are also downsides to WFH. For instance, many people reported a lack of distinction between their personal lives and their professional lives (and even their workspaces and their personal spaces). WFH also reduced serendipitous contact between employees, which in turn negatively affected creativity. Similarly, physical separation hindered employee camaraderie and impeded efforts to foster effective teams. Additionally, some remote workers perceived themselves to be "out of sight, out of mind" as this related to career advancement, thereby reducing morale and negatively impacting loyalty toward their organizations.[24]

Overall, however, the positives seem to have outweighed the negatives. As employees enjoyed new freedoms, and as governments issued direct payments to individuals and families, people felt empowered to retire early or take an unofficial sabbatical or even start a business of their own. They also left the aforementioned "toxic work cultures" that had plagued them before the pandemic. It may be argued that the "great resignation" had less to

23. Bick, "Work From Home," 1–15.
24. Madell, "7 Benefits," paras. 15–18.

do with people "quitting their jobs," than people reassessing their situations and using the disruption of the pandemic as an opportunity to reorder their lives.

This constellation of issues makes clear how daunting the prospect of effecting meaningful change can be and demonstrates the power of "mammon" to subjugate people on both a personal and a corporate level. For many in the workplace, however, it isn't merely the presence of mammon that is problematic; it is the crowding out of God that has left them both frustrated and spiritually bereft.

Creation, Abundance, and the Sovereignty of God

Among the concerns most commonly expressed by the conference's delegates was a general feeling that God has not only been eliminated from economic discourse but from economic consciousness. Business and other forms of economic activity are seen as radically secular, with no room for consideration of the divine or even religiously informed ethical constraint. Work is viewed primarily as a means of subsistence, a kind of "necessary evil," even among the very ambitious who see it as a means of acquiring great personal wealth. Rarely, however, is it understood as something sacred, something fundamental to the essence of our humanity or a potential source of human flourishing.

Similarly, most economic activity is based upon a presumption of scarcity. Competition for limited, and potentially insufficient, resources creates a "zero-sum game" mentality, where one person's gain inevitably results in another's loss; and the purpose of the "game" is to win at all costs, with little or no consideration of how one's economic decisions and/or actions impact other people, other communities, or the natural environment.

These things, of course, run counter to biblical teaching on the sovereignty of God and the nature of humankind, the abundance of God's provision, the meaning and purpose of work (and other forms of economic activity), and humanity's on-going role in the maintenance of God's creation (a.k.a. "the cultural mandate").

This misalignment is not only disconcerting for people of faith, but its memetic entrenchment also makes it very difficult to renew people's minds and transform their behavior for the benefit of all.

Human Frailty and the Effects of the Fall

As both the creation narratives and everyday experience tell us, humankind is morally deficient. Our inherent sinfulness leads us to the constant pursuit of personal pleasure and personal aggrandizement. Our daily actions betray a prejudice for self-satisfaction (often at the expense of others) over concern for the common good. This had led to everything from individual acts of deception to instances of endemic corruption and "the tragedy of the commons."[25]

The spiritual corruption of economic activity is as old as the story of Babel (Gen 11:1–9), and God's condemnation of economic excess, greed, injustice, malice, dishonesty, and moral turpitude harken back to the days of Sodom and Gomorrah (Gen 19:1–19), the revelation of the Decalogue (Exod 20:2–17), and the various ordinances of God found throughout the Torah (Deut 4:44—28:68).

Despite specific warnings against such depravity, humankind has continued down a path of personal and endemic corruption, with catastrophic consequences. One need only consider the long and dreadful history of human conquest, slavery, war, resource exploitation, famine, rebellion, revolution, and gender-based oppression to understand the futility of such behavior; yet it continues in one form or another, unabated. It is no wonder that many have grown weary of this reality, as information technologies and a twenty-four-seven news cycle bring their present-day manifestations to our attention on a daily basis.

The constant onslaught of "bad news" has contributed to a period of unprecedented cynicism, especially toward government,[26]

25. Hardin, "Tragedy of the Commons."
26. Pew Research Center, "Public Trust," paras. 1–11.

but cynicism simply isn't an option for people of faith who wish to see the redemption of our economic system. Firstly, in the world's largest economy (the United States), business is generally regarded more highly than government and is seen as a more probable agent for positive societal change than government.[27] Secondly, while keenly aware of human depravity and God's righteous judgment, people of faith are profoundly aware of God's incomparable grace and God's desire for the redemption of all things.

The Need for Economic Redemption

The following is noted by the author in a previous work:

> The Oxford Online Dictionary defines redemption as "the action of saving or being saved from sin, error, or evil." While the term is often used in reference to an individual's eternal state of grace (that is, salvation), it may also apply to any attempt at correcting errors of the past. One of the most important things to understand about redemption is that it is a process of healing, not a ready-made cure. It involves an acknowledgment of the past and the errors inherent therein, and it requires honest and probing assessments of past actions, their causes, and their effects. . . . Rather than formulating a quick fix to a problem that took generations to create, this [redemptive] approach seeks to transform our economic system by reclaiming the moral values that once undergirded it.[28]

The entire biblical epoch is the story of God's unrelenting redemption of God's creation, and particularly the redemption of humanity. It is the story of God's grace taking precedence over God's wrath. As the apostle Paul teaches in the Epistle to the Romans,

> God demonstrates his own love for us in this: While we were still sinners, Christ died for us. Since we have now

27. Edelman, "Trust Barometer," 5.
28. Barnes, *Redeeming Capitalism*, 90.

been justified by his blood, how much more shall we be saved from God's wrath through him! For if, while we were God's enemies, we were reconciled to him through the death of his Son, how much more, having been reconciled, shall we be saved through his life! Not only is this so, but we also boast in God through our Lord Jesus Christ, through whom we have now received reconciliation. (Rom 5:8–11 NIV)

Yet, while we live in the hope of God's redemptive mercies, we recognize that our current circumstances are still subject to the vagaries of the fall.

The reality of our "already but not yet"[29] existence presents a paradox for those seeking a more efficient, sustainable, and just economic system. On the one hand, we recognize the need for the magisterial restraint of evil and the effects of sin (i.e., the use of legislation and regulation to deter and sanction bad behavior). On the other hand, we seek a system that optimizes the benefits of free expression, risk and reward, and innovation that is unencumbered by overly proscriptive government interventions. To achieve the latter however, there must be universally accepted codes of conduct based upon generally agreed standards of moral and ethical behavior. Identifying those standards and gaining tacit agreement on them is no easy task, but it is not impossible.

Business Ethics

Again, as the author notes in a previous work:

> While no consensus exists on the particulars of right conduct, areas of common ground across all religious traditions, and even among those with no religious faith, make it possible to construct a business ethic that is universally applicable. All human beings, whether they acknowledge it or not, possess both the image of God (*imago Dei*) and a deep-seated sense of the divine

29. Ladd, *Presence of the Future.*

(*sensus divinitatis*) that are the very building blocks of what theologians call common grace.[30]

The former, is based upon the belief that despite human depravity, the imprimatur of the divine remains, rendering all people capable of right conduct. The latter, upon the belief that regardless of one's acceptance or rejection of God, both an inherent sense of divine presence and an innate desire to emulate God's nature (a.k.a. "God is love") will ultimately animate one's moral conscience. The author goes on to note:

> One need only consider the ethical foundations of various religious systems to quickly discern the commonality between them. Islam possesses many of the same beliefs about the ontology of ethics that Judaism and Christianity share, and all three Abrahamic faiths put a high premium on right conduct and moral discipline. Similarly, Hinduism and Buddhism, while not as proscriptive as the monotheistic faiths, highly value the development of virtue and the avoidance of vice. Likewise, Taoism and Confucianism place great emphasis on the development of good character and the desire to seek harmony and the common good. Even those who subscribe to moralistic atheism ground their beliefs in a kind of natural law based largely on human empathy and an evolutionary desire to protect the species. The net result is that people of faith need not fear the need to compromise their religious convictions in order to achieve common moral ground, and people without faith need not conclude that invocations of the divine necessarily constitute a hidden agenda of proselytization.[31]

The data above raise serious questions about the spiritual, intellectual, physical, emotional, and pastoral needs of people in the workplace. What are the personal challenges faced by employees and managers alike, and what, if any, are the unique challenges of people of faith? The delegates to the aforementioned conference

30. Barnes, *Redeeming Capitalism*, 117.
31. Barnes, *Redeeming Capitalism*, 118.

explored these topics as well and uncovered common themes across a wide cross section of industries and professions.

Christians in the Marketplace—What Do They Face and What Do They Need?

The challenges presented by the contemporary workplace are well documented. Many are shared by believers and nonbelievers alike. For the purposes of this study, particular attention will be given to the former while giving note to those phenomena that are experienced generally.

Loneliness and Isolation

Among the first challenges cited by delegates to the conference was a palpable sense of loneliness and isolation in the workplace. In a recent article by former US Surgeon General Vivek Murthy in Harvard Business Review, this problem was described as an "epidemic," with a negative health impact equivalent to smoking fifteen cigarettes per day.[32]

The causes of loneliness in the workplace are many, but it would appear that as workers become more connected "virtually" (i.e., via information technologies), they experience a greater sense of disconnection in "reality." Citing previous studies from the American Association of Retired People and Harvard Business, Murthy notes,

> We live in the most technologically connected age in the history of civilization, yet rates of loneliness have doubled since the 1980s. Today, over 40 percent of adults in America report feeling lonely, and research suggests that the real number may well be higher. Additionally, the number of people who report having a close confidante in their lives has been declining over the past few

32. Murthy, "Loneliness," para. 13.

decades. In the workplace, many employees—and half of CEOs—report feeling lonely in their roles.[33]

People of faith are not immune to this reality; in fact, they are often isolated *because* of their religious beliefs and/or affiliations. People of faith are often objectified in the workplace, either because of their outward expressions of faith and/or their lack of social conformity; or because of their unspoken expressions of faith, such as clothing, religious markings, religious observances, and other indicators of religious belief. While this is especially true for religious minorities, it is increasingly true for anyone who identifies as a "believer" of any kind, in the workplace.

It has been suggested by the Religious Freedom and Business Foundation that unfamiliarity with various religious traditions, and a misunderstanding of people's core values are at the heart of this phenomenon. Most companies, however, are reluctant to ask the hard questions necessary to bridge the gap between various belief systems for fear of unleashing further mistrust and suspicion between employees. As Johnson himself puts it,

> "WHY [*sic.*] do our coworkers do what they do at work? What are the work-related core beliefs and principles that they aspire to follow? It seems inappropriate to ask. Often, it feels like avenues for deeper connection are blocked. Our corporate culture is too fearful to let us truly connect. Management is worried that if we really knew one another's core motivations, we'd hate one another. It seems the presumption is that we can only "tolerate" each other from a distance; we can only work civilly together so long as we remain ignorant of our coworker's core identity. . . . We're worried that opening the "pandora's box" of religion and belief and core defining principles would cause chaos.[34]

There is considerable irony in this approach, as the research of McMillan and McCrindle, and others, would suggest that the best way to overcome loneliness in the workplace is to "shift the

33. Murthy, "Loneliness," para. 4.
34. Johnson, "Those People," para. 5.

focus from the worker experience to the human experience."[35] That is to say, organizations should treat their employees as "whole persons" (including their religious beliefs and values), and not as disembodied/disconnected human resources.

According to Johnson however, attitudes are beginning to change:

> Increasingly, corporate leaders, business school faculty members, social psychologists and HR consultants are extolling the benefits of full personal engagement, transparency and authenticity in the workplace. The time is ripe to take the next step toward truly valuing our employees for who they are, by championing their freedom of religion and belief. We can free workers to have deeper one-to-one connections in the workplace—connections across diverse cultures. Over time, those one-on-one relationships, built on personal knowledge and authentic connection . . . can help dissolve the barriers of distrust and suspicion that are strangling society today.[36]

Clearly, the combination of physical distance, mistrust, fear, and a lack of personal interaction have contributed to loneliness and isolation in the workplace; but those aren't the only factors negatively affecting believers in the workplace. Another factor, described by many delegates to the conference, is a general sense of insecurity—both job insecurity and diffidence over one's ability to personally contribute to the transformation of business culture(s).

Insecurity

Much has been written about the precarious nature of work in both standard and nonstandard settings. In the case of the latter, the nature of contract work itself is the primary cause of concern. The so-called gig economy is based purely on transactional utility, with little concern for the well-being of independent contractors. In the case of the former, there are many reasons why people are

35. McMillan, "Workplace Loneliness," 14.
36. Johnson, "Those People," para. 10.

concerned about their job security. Increased competition from abroad, the expanded use of stringent performance metrics, the decline of union representation, a geographically fluid employment pool, rapidly changing business processes, shifting demographics, and even the introduction of artificial intelligence (AI) have all contributed to an environment where employees are in constant fear of losing their jobs.

Prior to the impact of the COVID-19 pandemic described earlier, the power dynamic between employers and employees was so one sided that some employers even used the threat of redundancy as a perverse form of "motivation,"[37] to keep employees "on their toes," and more importantly, to keep them from disrupting the *status quo.*

It is a very brave person indeed who risks their livelihood to inform corporate culture along religiously inspired lines. Yet, it was Jesus himself who famously asked the question, "What good is it for someone to gain the whole world, yet forfeit their soul?" (Mark 8:36). Staying silent in the face of moral turpitude may seem expedient at the time, but as many will attest, to be complicit in wrongdoing can be both career limiting and soul destroying in the long run.

In a previous work, the author recounts the tragic story of a senior executive who had "lost everything," due in large part to his lack of moral courage. Someone steeped in religious belief and well versed in holy writ, following the "crowd" ultimately led him down a road to perdition, with devastating consequences. As the author explains,

> Sam was a mature student doing a DPhil at the Saïd Business School of Oxford University. It is not uncommon for mature students to attend business school. In fact, most students who attend are career executives from multinational companies seeking to enhance their careers by earning advanced professional degrees (typically an MBA). Sam's case however was rather different. Sam had already been a successful senior executive, but his career

37. Hassard, "Work-Related Stress."

and his life were left in ruins when he became involved in a high-profile business failure. He not only lost his job and his fortune, but he also lost his wife, his family and his sense of purpose in life. Sam had come to Oxford to start over. Sadly, things did not go very smoothly. . . . Sam's existence was a very lonely one and . . . Sam had never properly dealt with his immense loss or processed the magnitude of his grief. Instead, he pressed ahead with his studies and soon the pressures of academic life, coupled with his loneliness and unprocessed grief, were too much for him to bear, and instead of seeking help, he began to self-medicate by indulging in excessive amounts of alcohol.[38]

Sam was genuinely lost, and he knew that his own complicity in the company's immoral (and illegal) activities had led him to the pits of despair; and his guilt was palpable. Despite the efforts of many pastors, counselors, and medical professionals, he continued to drink heavily, putting his spiritual, emotional, and physical health in great jeopardy. He was a victim of both his company's corrupted culture and his own unwillingness to confront it.

Yet even those who are willing to take a stand against ethically compromised cultures sometimes doubt whether the risks they take, and the sacrifices they make, will have any lasting impact on individual and corporate behavior. So far has the pendulum swung toward "mammon," they perceive their experience to be a "clash of cultures."

Clash of Cultures

Across the faith, work and economics discipline, much attention has been paid to the so-called sacred/secular divide. Simply put, this expression seeks to define the compartmentalization of one's work life and one's spiritual life. In the United States it is rooted in a widely held belief that freedom *of* religion is tantamount to freedom *from* religion. It is generally supposed that religious belief

38. Barnes, *Dreaming Spires*, 74.

is a matter of personal preference and therefore has no place in nonreligious settings.

While pervasive, a purely secular approach to business and business ethics is not unassailable. As the author has previously noted,

> This approach is flawed for several reasons. First, secularism is itself a belief system and a worldview, and to suggest otherwise would be nonsensical. Second, as long as religion remains an important source of cultural identity and moral guidance, it will continue to influence business and business cultures. Finally, secularism presumes that economic pluralization and religious belief are somehow incompatible, but that is more an *a priori* assumption than a self-evident or established fact. . . . The global economy is a vast and complex constellation of powerful and influential businesses, capital, governments, organizations, and institutions, but it is also a vast network of individual people with minds, wills, and consciences. . . . As the traditional guardians of virtue, ethics, and morality, religious faiths are uniquely placed to influence the future of the global economy, not merely because faith communities have political strength in numbers, but because their traditional values still have currency in the marketplace of ideas.[39]

Sadly, many people of faith no longer feel safe sharing their moral convictions for fear of reprisal.

Anti-Religious Sentiment / Religious Persecution

The decline of religious observance in the West has been well documented for decades. So-called post-Christian Europe has been a phenomenon for much of the modern era, but until quite recently, the Unites States has bucked the trend. Since the turn of the millennium, however, religious observance in America has been in steep decline. According to a recent study by the Pew Research Center,

39. Barnes, *Redeeming Capitalism*, 118.

More than eight-in-ten members of the Silent Generation (those born between 1928 and 1945) describe themselves as Christians (84%), as do three-quarters of Baby Boomers (76%). In stark contrast, only half of Millennials (49%) describe themselves as Christians; four-in-ten are religious "nones," and one-in-ten Millennials identify with non-Christian faiths.[40]

With that decline has come a virulent form of atheism and religious persecution. The so-called New Atheism of Richard Dawkins, Sam Harris, Daniel Dennett, the late Christopher Hitchens, and others has sought not merely to refute religious belief but to eradicate it, on the grounds that it is inherently pernicious. The result has been a popular narrative that treats all religious systems as fundamentally intolerant, and by extension, people of faith as xenophobic, homophobic, racist, etc.

Consequently, nearly half of all Americans believe that Christians in America are being persecuted for their beliefs,[41] a situation that is hardly conducive to constructive dialogue. There appears to be little room, if any, for people of faith to express their opinions on business ethics without being castigated for their sexual ethics or some other tenet of faith that others may find objectionable. This is tantamount to a "heckler's veto," that effectively silences anyone who doesn't conform to the moral relativism of the era.

Moral Relativism

For the purposes of this study, it is not necessary to delve deeply into the metaethics of moral relativism, which as a vein of philosophical inquiry is vast and complex. It is sufficient to simply understand the drift in popular consciousness from generally accepted moral standards, such as truth-telling, honest dealing, and mutual concern for others (see the Golden Rule), to a presupposition that a lack of moral absolutes renders all ethical constraint extraneous.

40. Pew Research Center, "Decline of Christianity," 8.
41. Jones, "How Immigration," 16.

In such an environment, ethical egoism (i.e., the supremacy of self-interest over all other ethical considerations) is the only available construct for determining the morality of any business decision. This line of thinking is in direct conflict with the ethical underpinnings of most faith traditions, including Christianity. Christians in the workplace, often find themselves vociferously opposed when they seek to interject moral reasoning, based upon religious teachings; even those teachings that are literally engraved in the halls of judicial power. Not only does this further isolate people of faith in the workplace, but a lack of divergent views can create a hostile work environment for those who are ostracized or pressured to conform, and can even lead to the dangerous phenomenon of groupthink.

Groupthink

The term groupthink was famously coined by American sociologist William H. Whyte Jr. in a 1952 article for Fortune Magazine.[42] In the article he defines the phenomenon as a "rationalized conformity," whereby the consensus of a group becomes its over-riding consideration. There is little or no room for dissenting opinions if those opinions appear to be at odds with the prevailing mood. This has led to countless business, military, and societal failures that are well documented in both popular and academic journals. Nonetheless, it continues to plague organizations large and small and is especially common in cases of moral choice. People of conscience are often subjected to veiled threats of retaliation for seeking to "impose" their religious beliefs on others; and may even find themselves excluded from future decision making.

Such sanctions, both overt and covert, can create environments where Christians in the workplace become despondent and mourn the lack of affirmation they once felt in their jobs.

42. Whyte, "Groupthink," para 4.

Widespread Feelings of Loss

Participants at the conference expressed feelings of lament as it pertained to their overall well-being in the workplace. Many complained that they had lost trust in their superiors as well as their peers. They no longer felt safe expressing their beliefs, publicly or privately in the workplace. They couldn't be sure that others would "have their back" and defend their right to express a moral opinion based upon strongly held religious beliefs.

Many felt betrayed by an apparent loss of affection, even love, on the part of their colleagues and their organizations. They had indeed loved their work, their companies, their co-workers, their suppliers, and their customers, not in a mawkish sense but in a biblical sense. They were deeply committed to their mutual well-being and were willing to make great personal sacrifices toward mutually beneficial goals and objectives. That love has been eroded beyond recognition, as more noble business objectives have been totally supplanted by short-term financial metrics.

Instead of finding meaning and purpose at work, they increasingly find themselves resenting their participation in an economic system that creates excessive amounts of wealth for a few while exploiting the many, and significantly damaging the natural environment in the process. For some, who once found personal satisfaction in their work, the excesses of the system have presented them with a kind of identity crisis. "Who am I?" some asked. Am I an image bearer of the divine, whose work reflects the *imago Dei*, or am I merely a helpless cog in a money-churning machine, whose soulless march toward economic efficiency threatens my own spiritual well-being?

Feeling Spiritually Bereft

As Christians in the workplace find themselves in ever more hostile environments, they often succumb to the temptation to conform. As a measure of self-defense, or even survival, they collude in the compartmentalization of their own lives, until their faith becomes marginalized to the point of nominal influence. The fruit of the Spirit—love, joy, peace, patience, kindness, goodness, faithfulness, gentleness, and self-control (Gal 5:22–23)—are replaced by selfishness, melancholy, divisiveness, impatience, meanness, cynicism, crassness, and reactive, ill-considered behavior.

The exclusion of one's faith from activities that occupy most of one's waking hours can easily result in the relegation of God from an ever-present reality to an occasional consideration. Lost are regular rhythms of prayer and devotion; and work, instead of being one's "worship" (Rom 12:1), is nothing more than the means to a material end. Overworked, underappreciated, and faced with the regular prospect of moral tragedy[43] many Christians in the workplace report feelings of resentment, anger, helplessness, and overall dissatisfaction at work.

Research by McMillan has shown that dissatisfaction at work, and a lack of meaning and purpose, contribute to a vicious cycle of increased stress, reduced productivity, higher absenteeism, and generally toxic workplaces. Conversely, higher levels of job satisfaction, and workplaces that foster feelings of meaning and purpose, result in lower levels of stress, higher productivity, higher retention rates, and generally healthier workplaces. They also promote a better work/life balance, a benefit especially desirable among emerging generations.[44] Yet, companies persist in crowding out the spiritual feelings and needs of their employees.

An Endless Tunnel Without Light

It is not only in the spheres of business and industry, however, that mammon has sought to control the lives of the unsuspecting but in the everyday grind of daily life. Despite economic indicators of a relatively robust economy,[45] the majority of Americans report feel-

43. For the purposes of this work, "moral tragedy" shall be defined as participation in an action or decision that violates one's conscience or religious beliefs.

44. McMillan, "Workplace Loneliness."

45. At the time of writing, the S&P 500 was at an all-time high, the job

ing worse off and under greater financial strain than in the recent past. This is due to a variety of reasons that defy economic statistics. First among them is the high cost of food. While inflation may be going down, the initial impact of higher food prices (especially bread, eggs, and other grain-dependent staples) has been a shock to the system, as has the increase of both petrol and home heating fuels. When the cost of basic necessities become burdensome, no set of statistics will ameliorate the pain, or the fear, experienced by ordinary consumers. They influence every other financial consideration and increase overall levels of personal anxiety.

Likewise, the overall cost of housing has skyrocketed. With mortgage rates reflecting the Federal Reserve's monetary policies (i.e., increasing interest rates to stem inflation), it is more difficult for young homeowners to get on the "housing ladder." It also drives up demand for rental properties. As demand increases, so do rents, increasing housing insecurity across the country.[46] Homeowners have also seen significant increases in their costs, as local and state taxes have risen to keep up with both rising administrative costs and shifting demographics. Additionally, as the population ages, medical costs rise disproportionately to other costs, making life especially difficult for retirees living on fixed incomes. Meanwhile, younger families are struggling under mountains of both student debt and credit card debt, leaving few sectors of society unaffected by severe financial stress.[47] Like a tunnel with no light at its end, or a treadmill that never stops, millions of people feel trapped by "the system" and wondering what they can do to escape the so-called rat race.

And so, the unrelenting hegemony of "mammon" continues unabated, with catastrophic consequences for the health and well-being of real people. But there are other phenomena at work to

---

market was operating at "full employment," the inflation rate had gone from 9.1 percent to 3.4 percent in eighteen months, and pay increases are outpacing inflation.

46. Airgood-Obrycki et al., "State," para. 1.

47. Bhattarai, "Americans," para. 41.

enslave us and whose impact cannot be ignored. First among them is the two-edged sword of modern technology.

Bibliography

Airgood-Obrycki, Whitney, et al. *The State of the Nation's Housing*. Edited by Loren Berlin. Cambridge: Joint Center for Housing Stuides of Harvard University, 2023. https://www.jchs.harvard.edu/sites/default/files/reports/files/Harvard_JCHS_The_State_of_the_Nations_Housing_2023.pdf.

Balu, Nivedita. "Amazon Layoff Signals More Pain for Tech Sector as Recession Fears Mount." Reuters, Jan. 5, 2023. https://www.reuters.com/technology/amazon-layoff-signals-more-pain-tech-sector-recession-fears-mount-2023-01-05/.

Barnes, Kenneth J. *Light from the Dreaming Spires: Reflections on Ministry to Generation Y*. Eugene, OR: Resource, 2017.

———. *Redeeming Capitalism*. Grand Rapids: Eerdmans, 2018.

Barnes, Kenneth J., and John Hoffmire. "TrueFootprint, Ltd.: A Case Study in the Use of SME Innovation to Combat the COVID-19 Pandemic." *Journal of Ethics in Entrepreneurship and Technology* 1.1 (Apr. 2021). https://doi.org/10.1108/JEET-03-2021-0011.

Bhattarai, Abha. "Americans Tell Us Why They're Feeling Better—or Worse—About the Economy." *Washington Post*, Dec. 25, 2023. https://www.washingtonpost.com/business/2023/12/25/better-off-worse-off-economy/.

Bick, Alexander, et al., "Work from Home After the COVID-19 Outbreak." Federal Reserve Bank of Dallas, Working Paper 2017, July 2020. https://www.dallasfed.org/media/documents/research/papers/2020/wp2017.

Covey, Stephen M. R., et al. *Trust and Inspire: How Truly Great Leaders Inspire Greatness in Others*. New York: Simon & Schuster, 2022.

Cukierman, Alex. "COVID-19, Seignorage, Quantitative Easing and the Fiscal-Monetary Nexus." *Comparative Economic Studies* 63.2 (Apr. 13, 2021) 181–99. https://doi.org/10.1057/s41294-021-00150-7.

Edelman. "2018 Edelman Trust Barometer: Implications for CEOs." Annual Global Study. https://www.edelman.com/sites/g/files/aatuss191/files/2018-10/Edelman_Trust_Barometer_Implications_for_CEOs_2018.pdf.

Edwards, John. "Whatever Happened to Six Sigma?" *Information Week*, Aug. 16, 2022. https://www.informationweek.com/it-life/whatever-happened-to-six-sigma-.

Folger, Rorger, and Mary A. Konovsky. "Effects of Procedural and Distributive Justice on Reactions to Pay Raise Decisions." *Academy of Management* 32.1 (Mar. 1989) 115–30.]https://web.mit.edu/curhan/www/docs/Articles/15341_Readings/Justice/Folger.pdf.

Ford, Jeffrey D., et al. "Resistance to Change: The Rest of the Story." *Academy of Management Review* 33.2 (Apr. 1, 2008) 362–77. https://doi.org/10.5465/amr.2008.31193235.

Hall, John. "The Cost of Turnover Can Kill Your Business and Make Things Less Fun." *Forbes*, May 9, 2019. https://www.forbes.com/sites/johnhall/2019/05/09/the-cost-of-turnover-can-kill-your-business-and-make-things-less-fun/?sh=39e46daa7943.

Hardin, Garrett. "The Tragedy of the Commons: The Population Problem Has No Technical Solution; It Requires a Fundamental Extension in Morality." *Science* 162.3859 (Dec. 13, 1968) 1243–48. https://www.science.org/doi/10.1126/science.162.3859.1243.

Harrison, David. "How High Is Inflation and What Causes It? What to Know." *Wall Street Journal*, last updated Sept. 13, 2022. https://www.wsj.com/articles/inflation-definition-cause-what-is-it-11644353564.

Hassard J., et al. The Cost of Work-Related Stress to Society: A Systematic Review. *J Occup Health Psychol* 23.1 (Jan. 2018) 1–17. https://pubmed.ncbi.nlm.nih.gov/28358567/.

Insights. "Christians Are More Satisfied with Their Work-Life Balance." Oct. 20, 2016. https://www.insights.uca.org.au/christians-are-more-satisfied-with-their-work-life-balance/.

Jefferson, Thomas, et al. "Declaration of Independence (1776)." Last updated Sept. 20, 2022. https://www.archives.gov/milestone-documents/declaration-of-independence.

Johnson, Kent. "THOSE People Are Awful! But . . ." *Religious Freedom and Business Foundation*, Jan. 23, 2021. https://religiousfreedomandbusiness.org/2/post/2021/01/those-people-are-awful.html.

Jones, Mark. "COVID Response Drives $24 Trillion Surge in Global Debt: IIF." Reuters, Feb. 17, 2021. https://www.reuters.com/article/business/covid-response-drives-24-trillion-surge-in-global-debt-iif-idUSKBN2AH284/.

Jones, Robert P., et al. "How Immigration and Concerns About Cultural Changes Are Shaping the 2016 Election." PRRI/Brookings. June 23, 2016. https://www.prri.org/wp-content/uploads/2016/06/PRRI-Brookings-2016-Immigration-survey-report.pdf.

Ladd, George Eldon. *The Presence of the Future: The Eschatology of Biblical Realism.* Grand Rapids: Eerdmans, 1996.

Madell, Robin. "7 Benefits of Working From Home (and 7 Drawbacks)." *US News*, July 16, 2024. https://money.usnews.com/money/blogs/outside-voices-careers/articles/pros-and-cons-of-working-from-home.

McMillan, Lindsay. "Workplace Loneliness: Solutions for the Growing Epidemic." *Reventure.* 2019. https://ia803109.us.archive.org/0/items/6185752-Workplace-Loneliness-Report/6185752-Workplace-Loneliness-Report.pdf.

Murthy, Vivek. "Work and the Loneliness Epidemic: Reducing Isolation at Work Is Good for Business." *Harvard Business Review*, Sept. 26, 2017. https://hbr.org/2017/09/work-and-the-loneliness-epidemic.

Nix, Adam, et al. "Enron and the California Energy Crisis: The Role of Networks in Enabling Organizational Corruption." *Business History Review* 95.4 (2021) 765–802. doi:10.1017/S0007680521001008.

Pew Research Center. "In U.S., Decline of Christianity Continues at Rapid Pace: An Update on America's Changing Religious Landscape." Oct. 17, 2019. https://www.pewresearch.org/religion/2019/10/17/in-u-s-decline-of-christianity-continues-at-rapid-pace/.

Pew Research Center. "Public Trust in Government: 1958–2024." June 24, 2024. https://www.pewresearch.org/politics/2024/06/24/public-trust-in-government-1958–2024/.

Pope, Hugh. "Mammon." *The Catholic Encyclopedia*. Vol. 9. New York: Robert Appleton, 1910. http://www.newadvent.org/cathen/09580b.htm.

Rehman, Nabeel, et al. "The Psychology of Resistance to Change: The Antidotal Effect of Organizational Justice, Support and Leader-Member Exchange." *Frontiers in Psychology* 12 (2021) 1–15. https://doi.org/10.3389/fpsyg.2021.678952.

Rodrigues, Jorge José Martins, and Nelson José dos Santos António. "Manager's Entrenchment, Power and Corporate Governance." *Euro Asia Journal of Management* 21.40 (2011) 39–50.

Shankar, Kameshwari, et al. "Evidence on Online Higher Education: The Promise of COVID-19 Pandemic Data." *Management and Labour Studies* 48.2 (2023) 242–49. https://doi.org/10.1177/0258042X211064783.

Sull, Donald, et al. "Toxic Culture Is Driving the Great Resignation." *MIT Sloan Management Review*, Jan. 11, 2022. https://sloanreview.mit.edu/article/toxic-culture-is-driving-the-great-resignation/.

Tanner, Tom. "Online Learning at ATS Schools: Part 1—Looking Back at Our Past." Association of Theological Schools. Feb. 2017. https://www.ats.edu/files/galleries/online-learning-part-1.pdf.

Whyte, William H., Jr. "Groupthink." *Fortune*, Feb. 29, 1952. https://fortune.com/article/groupthink-fortune-1952/.

Xu, Yin, and Yike Wang. "Job Stress and University Faculty Members' Life Satisfaction: The Mediating Role of Emotional Burnout." *Frontiers in Psychology* 14 (2023) 1–10. https://doi.org./10.3389/fpsyg.2023.1111434.

Zweig, Ben, and Daniel Zhao. "Looking for Greener Pastures: What Workplace Factors Drive Attrition?" Glassdoor June 9, 2021. https://www.glassdoor.com/blog/employee-attrition-drivers/.

Chapter Two

Prometheus Ascending
From the Atom Bomb to AI

Kenneth J. Barnes

Few are probably aware that Mary Shelley's famous novel *Frankenstein* has an alternative title: *The Modern Prometheus*. Prometheus, of course, was the Titan of Greek mythology, who defied the Olympian Gods by stealing fire (the most primitive form of technology) and giving it to humans. The penalty for his impertinence was perpetual torture, but the consequence of his action was the human propensity to deploy technology beyond humanity's ability to control it.

As Henri Nouwen noted in *The Wounded Healer*, this is a universal fear that has discomfited humankind for millennia. He recounts the ancient tale of four Indian princes who traveled the world seeking knowledge at the edges of science. The first had discovered a method for reconstituting the flesh of a living creature from nothing more than a fragment of bone. The second said that he had learned how to grow skin and hair on such a creature's flesh. The third claimed the ability to grow its limbs, while the fourth

33

pronounced his ability to give its reconstituted body life. Setting out to find a bone upon which to work their newfound skills, they unwittingly recreated a lion, who, upon receiving its animation, turned on the princes, devouring them all.[1]

These are ancient myths that reflect a contemporary truth. With each new technological advance comes both the opportunity to improve the quality of human life and the potential to destroy it. The power rests not with the technologies themselves but with the human agents who employ them.

While an age-old concern, technophobia was heightened during the Industrial Revolution, when the harnessing of steam power led to the creation of machines that seriously threatened the livelihoods of skilled workers and craftsmen. Over time, however, it became clear that, while the temporary effects of labor displacement may be quite detrimental to individuals in the short term, overall, societies that employed new tools and methods created unprecedented amounts of wealth and, with that wealth, came vast improvements in overall living conditions. Those who opposed the never-ending "march of progress" were often derided as "Luddites," a sardonic reference to axe-wielding dissidents who attempted to thwart the deployment of new technologies by attacking the machines themselves. Despite the rise of fleeting counter movements such as nineteenth century Romanticism and the Arts and Crafts Movement of the early twentieth century, people have generally accepted and even embraced technological advancement. The twentieth century, however, did give rise to two very notable exceptions: the devastating effects of mechanized warfare experienced during World War I and the unprecedented use of nuclear weapons at the close of World War II.

World War I, or the Great War as it is known across Europe, was supposed to be "the war to end all wars."[2] So ruinous was its effects that politicians, academics, social commentators, and everyday citizens alike were sure that humankind had had its fill

1. Nouwen, *Wounded Healer*, 5.
2. This sobriquet is based on the title of the book by H. G. Wells, *The War That Will End War* (1914).

of death, destruction, and warring madness.[3] The efficiencies of modern, mechanized warfare were nearly beyond comprehension. While exact figures are difficult to ascertain, it is estimated that between 1914 and 1918, twenty million people died as a direct result of the war. The Ottoman Empire alone lost 20 percent of its male population, while France and Germany lost approximately 10 percent of theirs. In a conflict that ended in a virtual stalemate, the world never truly recovered from the physical, emotional, and spiritual damage inflicted upon combatants and civilians alike. Within a generation, however, the world was once again at war, and the technology employed to end it has cast a long and ominous shadow over the future of humanity itself.

The Plight of Nuclear Man

In some ways it would not be inappropriate to mark time as BB (before the bomb) and AB (after the bomb), so tenuous is the plight of humankind since the development and deployment of the first nuclear weapons in 1945. The work of thousands of scientists at a cost of 2 billion USD (a staggering amount at the time) produced a technology so powerful that, for the first time in human history, *homo sapiens* were not only capable of taking human life but of eliminating human life altogether. It is almost too horrific to contemplate the enormity of that fact, and yet we must remain cognizant of it, at all times. Otherwise, we run the risk of inuring ourselves to the ever-present reality that it only takes one miscalculation, or one insane decision, to induce our own annihilation. It is, in fact, the guarantee of mutually assured destruction (MAD) that has deterred world leaders from deploying nuclear weapons for decades; but one wonders whether that presumption will ultimately prove effective in the long run. As recently as February 2024, Russian President Vladimir Putin raised the specter of nuclear war, including the possibility of a "first strike" should

---

3. The term "warring madness" is taken from a hymn entitled "God of Grace and God of Glory" by Rev. Harry Emerson Fosdick, a Baptist minister and WWI chaplain.

Western troops be deployed in the defense of Ukraine,[4] and accounts of the Cuban Missile Crisis of 1962 remind us of how close we've already come to a devastating miscalculation.[5]

And so, we live with a nuclear sword of Damocles over our collective heads, creating a psychological framework that Nouwen calls "the predicament of nuclear man."[6] Unlike any previous generation, we who live in the late modern period face not merely an uncertain future but an "optional" future, wherein the genius of our own technology may hasten our own demise. So obtrusive is this subconscious reality that we have become "historically dislocated" without a clear reference to either the foundational assumptions of the past or the promise of a brighter future. We have lost connection with the metanarrative that guided previous generations and find ourselves floundering in a morass of pitiless monotony. We have laws without values, transactions without commitments, ideas without ideologies, respite without rest, and death without hope of resurrection.

According to Nouwen, this has led "nuclear man" to seek a "new immortality" either through transcendental means or the path of revolution. The former seeks it by way of escape from the reality of a doomed material existence, the latter, from the creation of a new world order, unencumbered by the strictures of previous social arrangements. "His goal is not a better man, but a new man, a man who relates to himself and the world in ways which are still unexplored, but which belong to his hidden potentials."[7] Or, as technology makes possible today, a total retreat into virtual reality (VR) where we willingly trick our senses into confusing what "is" with what "appears to be" because what "is" seems unbearable.

VR technology made the leap from science fiction to science fact in the 1960s with the introduction of a multisensory

---

4. Soldatkin and Osborn, "Putin Warns West," para. 1.
5. Schlesinger, "Post Mortem on Cuba."
6. Nouwen, *Wounded Healer*, 5.
7. Nouwen, *Wounded Healer*, 18.

mechanical device called the Sensorama,[8] which merely sought to create an immersive theatrical experience. As digital computing has progressed, however, the ability to produce more lifelike experiences has begun to blur the lines between what is real and what is artificial, with millions of people regularly escaping into fantasy worlds of their own, where time and space are unencumbered by matter, choices are free of consequences, relationships are solely self-gratifying, and instant gratification subverts the need for meaning or purpose. But neither escapism nor efforts to technologically enhance humanity end there, as advances in the use of Artificial Intelligence threaten our traditional understanding of what it means to be human.

Artificial Intelligence and the Obsolescence of the Human Mind

Space here does not permit even a cursory review of the evolution from analog to digital technologies, or the more dramatic jump from digital to quantum computing, but the sheer size of data sets and the speed with which they may be analyzed has created a world where machines may be "taught to think" (so-called artificial general intelligence) and create content through the use of artificial neural networks (so-called generative artificial intelligence). Both of these technologies have tremendous potential as tools designed to improve the human condition; however, they also have the potential to render the human mind obsolete. As Pope Francis states quite accurately,

> All of us are called to grow together, in humanity and as humanity. . . . We are called to reflect carefully on the theoretical development and the practical use of these new instruments of communication and knowledge. Their great possibilities for good are accompanied by the risk of turning everything into abstract calculations that reduce individuals to data, thinking to a mechanical process, experience to isolated cases, goodness to profit, and,

8. Heilig, "Sensorama Simulator."

above all, a denial of the uniqueness of each individual and his or her story. The concreteness of reality dissolves in a flurry of statistical data.[9]

Furthermore, the technologies in question are being created at speeds that even their developers fear could lead to unintended consequences, including the concentration of immense power in the hands of very few (and potentially bad) actors. As Dr. Anders Sandberg, Senior Research Fellow of the Future of Humanity Institute (University of Oxford), noted in a recent interview, artificial general intelligence

> is a very worthy goal to be pursuing. I just wish we were pursuing it a little bit more carefully. As somebody who was working in the world of neural networks, I'm surprised by the recent progress. And many people inside the field are also shocked and surprised by how rapidly things are moving. [They are moving] a bit more rapidly than is comfortable. Artificial intelligence, if it is as powerful as we believe . . . means that the company that actually gets self-improving AI might have . . . tremendous power over the world. . . . OpenAI and . . . Google DeepMind and Anthropic and . . . Microsoft and all the others—they sit on tremendous power and potentially they could get way more power.[10]

How much more powerful remains to be seen, but as we have witnessed with other, far less formidable technologies, unintended consequences can pose existential threats to humanity, while simultaneously destroying the human soul. One such example is technology's contribution to environmental degradation.

Confronting the Anthropocene

While from a strictly geological standpoint it is incorrect for one to refer to the current epoch as the Anthropocene, for many environmental scientists, the term has been appropriate for decades, if

9. Francis, "World Day of Social Communications," para 9.

10. Murgia, "Transcript," para. 73.

not centuries.[11] From at least the time of the Industrial Revolution, and perhaps as far back as the domestication of bovines, the impact of *homo sapiens* on the planet has been extraordinary. From the depletion of natural resources to the pollution of air and sea, from the extinction of species and the destruction of their natural habitats to the melting of the polar ice caps, the unbridled quest for economic growth has done irreparable damage to the planet and threatens the very existence of humanity. This is not only a scientific or sociological problem, but also a theological problem.

In her wonderful book entitled *Stewards of Eden*, biblical scholar Dr. Sandra L. Richter reminds her readers that our responsibility to steward God's creation harkens back to the creation narratives themselves. In reference to the second narrative (Gen 2:15) she states,

> The garden belongs to Yahweh, but human beings have been given the privilege to rule and the responsibility to care for this garden under the authority of their divine lord. This was the ideal plan, a world in which humanity (' *ādām*) would succeed in building human civilization in the midst of God's kingdom by directing and harnessing the amazing resources of this planet under the wise direction of their Creator. Moreover, as those made in the image of God, humanity is literally "installed" in the garden for this very task. Here there would always be enough. Progress would not necessitate pollution. Expansion would not require extinction. The privilege of the strong would not demand the deprivation of the weak.[12]

But of course, as with all of creation, our sinful rebellion has had devastating effects both on ourselves and our environment. Centuries of fossil fuel usage, chemical waste disposal, the ubiquitous use of plastics, the prodigious overconsumption of meat and the never-ending production of useless, disposable products has not only left behind a trail of environmental destruction, but it has

11. Amos, "Anthropocene."

12. Richter, *Stewards of Eden*, loc. 253.

also driven an economic system that exploits the poor, rewards greed and excess, and feeds an insatiable desire for personal pleasure and individual aggrandizement.

Ironically, in the very same narratives, God gives humanity the perfect model of moderation, reflection, and renewal by which to emulate the One whose image we bear, but we have ignored the gift of Sabbath to our physical, mental, emotional, and spiritual detriment.

Bibliography

Amos, Jonathan. "Anthropocene Unit of Geological Time Is Rejected." *BBC*, Mar. 21, 2024. https://www.bbc.com/news/science-environment-68632086.

Francis. "Message of His Holiness Pope Francis for the 58th World Day of Social Communications." Vatican website. Jan. 24, 2024. https://www.vatican.va/content/francesco/en/messages/communications/documents/20240124-messaggio-comunicazioni-sociali.html.

Heilig, M. L. "Sensorama Simulator." Patent Images. Aug. 28, 1962. https://patentimages.storage.googleapis.com/90/34/2f/24615bb97ad68e/US3050870.pdf.

Murgia, Madhumita, et al. "Transcript: Superintelligent AI—Transhumanism Etc." *Financial Times*, Dec. 5, 2023. https://www.ft.com/content/14123e16-25ab-45f1-912d-34ffcfoc8177.

Nouwen, Henry. *The Wounded Healer.* Garden City, NY: Doubleday, 1970.

Richter, Sandra L. *Stewards of Eden: What Scripture Says About the Environment and Why It Matters.* Downers Grove, IL: IVP Academic, 2020. Kindle.

Schlesinger, Arthur, Jr. "Post Mortem on Cuba: Memorandum from Schlesinger to the President." Oct. 29, 1962. https://nsarchive2.gwu.edu/nsa/cuba_mis_cri/19621029mortem.pdf.

Soldatkin, Vladimir, and Andrew Osborn. "Putin Warns West of Risk of Nuclear War, Says Moscow Can Strike Western Targets." Feb. 29, 2024. https://www.reuters.com/world/europe/putin-warns-west-risk-nuclear-war-says-moscow-can-strike-western-targets-2024-02-29/.

Chapter Three

Homo Obsessus
Humans Under Siege

KENNETH J. BARNES

A Mental Health Crisis

A RECENT REPORT BY the BBC noted that more than fifty thousand Americans committed suicide in 2023 (the most on record for a single year), and among people under the age of 35, it is the second leading cause of death.[1]

According to the Anxiety and Depression Association of America,

> Generalized Anxiety Disorder (GAD) is characterized by persistent and excessive worry about a number of different things. People with GAD may anticipate disaster and may be overly concerned about money, health, family, work, or other issues. Individuals with GAD find

1. Vernon, "Suicide," paras. 7, 26.

it difficult to control their worry. They may worry more than seems warranted about actual events or may expect the worst even when there is no apparent reason for concern.[2]

The National Institute of Mental Health defines depression as "a common but serious mood disorder. It causes severe symptoms that affect how a person feels, thinks, and handles daily activities, such as sleeping, eating, or working."[3]

According to the World Health Organization, the prevalence of both is on the rise, exacerbated by the impact of the COVID-19 pandemic.[4] A recent report by the Pew Charitable Trust states,

> Our nation is facing a new public health threat. Accelerated but not solely caused by the COVID-19 pandemic, feelings of anxiety and depression have grown to levels where virtually no one can ignore what is happening. A CNN/Kaiser Family Foundation poll put a number to it: 90% of Americans feel we are in a mental health crisis. They are right. A report in JAMA Health Forum has noted that 38% more people are in mental health care since the onset of the pandemic than before. And an unprecedented White House report from earlier this year begins, "Our nation is facing a mental health crisis among people of all ages, and the COVID-19 pandemic has only made these problems worse."[5]

The report goes on to describe three interrelated phenomena: youth mental health (a recent CDC study reported a staggering increase in the number of youths feeling sad or hopeless); serious mental illness (which reportedly reduces life expectancy by twenty to twenty-five years); and substance use disorder (which has resulted in a fivefold increase in drug-related deaths over the last twenty years).[6] This potent cocktail of despair requires im-

---

2. ADAA, "Generalized Anxiety Disorder," para. 1.
3. NIH, "Depression," para. 1.
4. WHO, "COVID-19 Pandemic."
5. Insel, "America's Mental Health Crisis," para. 1.
6. Insel, "America's Mental Health Crisis."

mediate attention on the part of both healthcare providers and governments, from both the private sector and the public sector; but it also requires the intervention of other "wellness" providers and caregivers, including friends, families, and religious communities. As the Pew research notes, preemptive action in the form of engagement with those who suffer is a very useful remedy; but our healthcare system isn't designed to offer faith, hope, and love; our religious traditions, though, are.

A Lack of Faith, Hope, and Love

In his recently published book entitled *Whatever Became of Love: An Invitation to Re-think Everything*, pastor-theologian Thomas C. Pfizenmaier speaks of a "contagion of separation"[7] at the root of humanity's ills. Our separation from God, from nature, from loved ones, from neighbors, from friends, from civil society and, yes, from communities of faith has left humanity in a Nietzschean dystopia where lost and hurting people have nowhere to turn; or so it seems to them. In a world where the spiritual has given way to the material, there is no room for faith and, where meaning and purpose have given way to utility and instant gratification, there is no room for hope. When relationships become mere transactions, there is no room for love; and in a world without love, there is nothing of enduring value for which to live.

Insatiability and an Addiction to Things

Unmoored by a sense of belonging to anything bigger than oneself, it is tempting to seek satisfaction through the pursuit of pleasure and the attainment of temporal goods. St. Augustine of Hippo (354–430 CE) recalls in his *Confessions* how his "unwell soul" led him into a "cauldron of unholy loves" and a craving for "objects of sense," resulting only in "jealousy, fear, suspicion, anger and strife." He "craved, through an excess of vanity, to be thought elegant and

---

7. Pfizenmaier, *Whatever Became of Love*, 33.

urbane," but his insatiable appetites only led him down a road to perdition and a "foul and dishonorable" life.[8]

Similarly, St. Thomas Aquinas (1225–74 CE) in his *Summa Theologiae* wrote extensively on humanity's relentless and futile quest for "happiness" through the pursuit of wealth, power, honor, fame, and pleasure. Their fleeting attainment only fuels the fires of insatiable desire, condemning the soul to an infinite cycle of fleeting reward and unfulfilled passions.[9] Or as the Bible says, "There are three words to describe the greedy: 'Give me more!' There are some things that are never satisfied. Forever craving more, they're unable to say, 'That's enough!'" (Prov 30:15 TPT).

In fact, while all the so-called global religions (Judaism, Christianity, Islam, Buddhism, Hinduism, and Confucianism), warn against the insatiability of temporal pursuits, denizens of late-modern, Western cultures suffer from more addictions than ever before. As noted earlier, drug addiction is at an all-time high, and alcohol-use disorder is rampant, especially among young people.[10] Problem gambling is developing into both a serious health crisis and a serious economic crisis.[11] And "binge behaviors," involving everything from food to television to pornography to smart phones are all on the rise.[12]

Such behaviors infringe on every part of our lives. They invade our spaces; they steal our time; they damage our relationships; they distort our values; they threaten our souls.

"Stop the World, I Want to Get Off"

The 1961 musical *Stop the World, I Want to Get Off* by Leslie Bricusse and Anthony Newly tells the story of a man whose relentless search for "more" leads him down countless dead ends and

8. Augustine, *Confessions*, 3.1.

9. Aquinas, *Summa Theologiae*, II.2.

10. National Institute on Alcohol Abuse and Alcoholism, "Alcohol Use in the United States."

11. Jones, "'We're Killing the Youth.'"

12. Flayelle and Lannoy, "Binge Behaviors."

cul-de-sacs of disappointment. Beginning with his birth, his life story unfolds, and at every overwhelming juncture, he symbolically "stops the world" (the character "breaks the fourth wall" and addresses the audience directly) so that he may reassess his circumstances and make yet another fateful decision. Toward the end of his life, as he writes his memoirs, he realizes that his relentless pursuit of pleasure and fortune was a terrible waste, and he comes to the startling conclusion that he had once possessed but tragically lost the only true love of his life. The play ends as he seeks redemption by sacrificing what is left of his own life to save that of his grandson. Miming his own birth, the audience is reminded of the play's beginning and is left wondering whether his grandson will repeat the man's mistakes or learn the man's lessons.

Introduced at a time when the aforementioned "nuclear man" was coming to terms with humanity's self-induced tribulations, the play, and the sentiments of its eponymous title, struck a chord in popular culture. It soon became a catchphrase for a general sense that things are moving too quickly, people are confused, and life itself, is out of control. Ironically, despite the main character's propensity for making disastrous decisions, the belief that there is innate wisdom in "stopping" rings true to even a casual observer.

As the pressures of postmodern capitalism, secularization, technological hegemony, emotional distress, loneliness, hopelessness, and social discord prevail, humanity is in great need of resilience; and there is no better source of that resilience than the ancient practice and divine gift of Sabbath.

Bibliography

Anxiety and Depression Association of America (ADAA). "Generalized Anxiety Disorder." Last updated Oct. 25, 2022. https://adaa.org/understanding-anxiety/generalized-anxiety-disorder-gad.

Aquinas, Thomas. *The Summa Theologiae of St. Thomas Aquinas*. Rev ed. Translated by the Fathers of the English Dominican Province. 1920. Revised by Kevin Knight. 2017. https://www.newadvent.org/summa/.

Augustine. *The Confessions*. Translated by J. G. Pilkington. From vol. 1 of *Nicene and Post-Nicene Fathers*, First Series. Edited by Philip Schaff. Buffalo,

NY: Christian Literature, 1887. Revised by Kevin Knight. http://www.newadvent.org/fathers/1101.htm.

Flayelle, Maèva, and Séverine Lannoy. "Binge Behaviors: Assessment, Determinants, and Consequences." *Addictive Behaviors Reports* 14 (2021) 1–3. https://doi.org/10.1016/j.abrep.2021.100380.

Insel, Thomas. "America's Mental Health Crisis." Pew. Dec. 8, 2023. https://www.pewtrusts.org/en/trend/archive/fall-2023/americas-mental-health-crisis.

Jones, Callum. "'We're Killing the Youth of America': Calls Grow for Crackdown on US Gambling." *Guardian*, Dec. 1, 2023. https://www.theguardian.com/us-news/2023/dec/01/sports-betting-regulation-gambling-addiction.

National Institutes of Health (NIH). "Depression." https://www.nimh.nih.gov/health/topics/depression.

National Institute on Alcohol Abuse and Alcoholism. "Alcohol Use in the United States: Age Groups and Demographic Characteristics." Last updated Sept. 2024. https://www.niaaa.nih.gov/alcohols-effects-health/alcohol-topics/alcohol-facts-and-statistics/alcohol-use-united-states-age-groups-and-demographic-characteristics.

Pfizenmaier, Thomas C. *Whatever Became of Love: An Invitation to Rethink Everything*. Eugene, OR: Resource, 2023.

Vernon, Will. "Suicide Is on the Rise for Young Americans, with No Clear Answers." *BBC*, Apr. 11, 2024. https://www.bbc.com/news/world-us-canada-68782177.

World Health Organization (WHO). "COVID-19 Pandemic Triggers 25% Increase in Prevalence of Anxiety and Depression Worldwide." Mar. 2, 2022. https://www.who.int/news/item/02-03-2022-covid-19-pandemic-triggers-25-increase-in-prevalence-of-anxiety-and-depression-worldwide.

Chapter Four

Sabbath as Resilience

KENNETH J. BARNES AND C. SARA LAWRENCE MINARD

A New Understanding of Biblical Sabbath

When one hears the word "apology" it is normative to think of an act of contrition. "I'm sorry," one might say, when asked to make an apology, even though the word itself is derived from the Greek apologia (ἀπολογία), meaning "to give an account" (i.e., explain). Over time, the common association of contrition with explanation came to change the meaning of the word itself, at least in common parlance.

The same may be said for the word Sabbath. While normally associated with the noun Sabbath (i.e., the Judeo-Christian "day of rest") or even the verb "rest"[1] itself, the word Sabbath (שָׁבַת) actually means "to cease." Its common usage being derived from its association with the aforementioned religious ordinance and its accompanying constraints (Exod 31:13–17).

Why does the change in word meaning matter? It matters because the common use of the word has obfuscated its intention

---

1. The more common word for rest in Hebrew is נוּחַ (*nuakh*).

47

and direction within the metanarrative of the biblical epoch. Far from being a mere injunction against manual labor or other forms of "work," as it is often understood, the biblical use of Sabbath is far more encompassing. As Autumn Ridenour, Mockler Professor of Christian Ethics at Gordon Conwell Theological Seminary, explains, humans

> are spiritual creatures meant for sabbath rest that reflects eternity as "gathered time." Sabbath directs humans to participate in the disruption of time demanded by the monotony of work, particularly in a digital age. By practicing Sabbath, we participate in a posture of receiving rather than producing, consuming, or performing alone. Instead, we receive our primary identity as persons made in the divine image and likeness who are redeemed as children of God.[2]

This broader understanding of Sabbath, presents a biblical construct of "Sabbath as prism," through which one may view, and better understand, the cosmic purpose and value of all human activity. Seen this way, Sabbath becomes a faith-based practice that readies the heart and mind and builds the resilience needed to challenge cultural norms present in business and economics by

a. prioritizing meaningful exchange over material gain,

b. seeing time as more than a utility function,

c. trusting in wonder and imagination more than command and control,

d. valuing people as more than a form of social currency, and

e. acknowledging God as the source of merit over the so-called self-made man or woman.

To better understand this notion of Sabbath as a prism, one must be willing to revisit the creation narratives in the book of Genesis, which suggest upon closer reading that Sabbath is more than merely the cessation of God's creative activities but the very

---

2. Ridenour, *Sabbath Rest as Vocation*, 159.

purpose and pinnacle of those activities. Or, as the Jewish scholar Abraham Heschel wrote, "The Sabbath is not for the sake of the weekdays, the weekdays for the sake of Sabbath. It is not an interlude but the climax of living."[3]

In Gen 1:2, one reads of God himself "at work," creating (*bara*/בּרא) *ex nihilo* and purely by force of will everything that exists (i.e., "the heavens and the earth"), thereby establishing God alone as the supreme sovereign over all of creation. In subsequent verses however (Gen 1:3–13), God divides his creation into several subordinate "kingdoms"—specifically, the kingdoms of day and night (day 1), water and sky (day 2), and earth (day 3). In Gen 1:14–31, God creates subordinate "rulers" to rule over these vassal kingdoms—namely, the sun and moon (day 4), fish and birds (day 5), and animals, including a unique species created "in the image of God," humankind (day 6).

Upon the completion of these lesser kingdoms and their rulers, God declares all this work to be "very good" (Gen 1: 31), and in Gen 2:1–2, God "ceases" (*shavot/sabbath* שָׁבַת) to work.[4] But of course, the story doesn't end there. In Gen 2:3, God proceeds to consecrate (*qadesh*/קָדַשׁ—i.e., make "holy") the seventh day, as a memorial to all God has done in creation, establishing it as both a testament to God's suzerainty and a paradigm for all subsequent economic activity. Day 7 is indeed "the Lord's Day," in that it points not only to the work of God but to the God of work.

This suzerain/vassal (superior king/lesser king) model is the framework for an entire hermeneutic of Scripture, commonly referred to as "covenant theology."[5] Through it, one comes to under-

3. Heschel, *Sabbath*, 14.

4. All Scripture quotations in this chapter are taken from the NIV.

5. Historically, the "macro" covenants of Scripture are understood as follows: the covenant of "redemption" (a pretemporal, prelapsarian concord within the Trinity itself, securing the means of salvation for humankind, despite human rebellion and depravity); the covenant of "works" (a temporal, prelapsarian settlement between God and humankind, represented by our biological antecedents, Adam and Eve); the covenant of "grace" (a temporal, postlapsarian set of concordats between God and humankind, administered through a series of "micro" covenants between God and Adam, God and Noah,

stand the being (i.e., "God is king," Ps 47:6–7), nature (i.e., "God is love," 1 John 4:8b), and character (i.e., "God is just," Dan. 9:14) of God, as well as the purpose of our relationship with God and the arc of redemptive history.

Under the covenant pericopes,[6] a broader understanding of Sabbath points toward humanity's role in the administration of God's kingdom and properly aligns human motives, and human actions, with God's divine plan. So, what is this divine plan?

As it relates to economic activity and work in particular, the Bible teaches that part of humankind's very purpose for being is to work in (abad/עָבַד) and preserve (shamar/שָׁמַר) God's creation (Gen 2:5–15) and to both flourish (i.e., be "fruitful"/parah/פָּרָה) and multiply (rabah/רָבָה)—the so-called "cultural mandate" (Gen 1: 28). In this prelapsarian state was great abundance (Gen 2: 9–16) and even the anticipation of the need for the future monetization of economic exchange (Gen 2:11–12). But there was one caveat: humankind was to stay in its lane, so to speak, and not try to "be like God," by partaking of the fruit of the "tree of the knowledge of good and evil" (Gen 2:17; 3:22). But humankind has always wanted to be like God, and therein lies the great cause of human suffering. This delusion has cost us by alienating us from God, and humanity's failure to recognize this hubris has perverted the very things for which we were created, such as work and other forms of economic activity (Gen 3:1–24).

This is evidenced in the earliest postlapsarian narratives: the story of Cain and Abel (Gen 4:1–18), the wickedness of humankind in the days of Noah (Gen 6:5–6), the story of the Tower of Babel (Gen 11:1–9), the famine in Canaan (Gen 12:10), and the destruction of Sodom and Gomorrah (Gen 19:1–28), continuing through to the exodus, where despite God's law being delivered to the people for their own protection (Exod 20–24), they continued to rebel against God's sovereignty, and to the end of the

God and Abraham, God and Moses, and God and David, and culminating in the new covenant of Jesus Christ, which ultimately secures our salvation and fulfills God's own covenant of redemption).

6. A pericope is a set of verses that forms one coherent unit or thought.

book of Judges, where the words of the chronicler say it all: "In those days, there was no king in Israel, and everyone did what was right in his own eyes" (Judg 21:25). Where human societies are concerned, over the ensuing 3,500 years, we still struggle to acknowledge God's sovereignty and, regardless of higher levels of human development, people still behave in lawless, unethical, and immoral ways in all spheres—and particularly in business, finance, and economics, where the ability to separate faith from fortune is often encouraged.

Framing Sabbath as Resilience

When combined with the economic and social pressures discussed in previous chapters, the cumulative effects of human depravity, organizational corruption, and moral tragedy can have profoundly negative effects on peoples' physical, mental, and spiritual well-being. It is generally accepted that, in order to cope with these negative effects and deal with unprecedented levels of stress and uncertainty, people need to increase their resilience, giving rise to a new milieu within the business management sector.[7]

Resilience refers to the ability to positively adapt to adversity and develop "readiness" for uncertain or unknown circumstances.[8] Not enough resilience can mean we break under pressure, and too much resilience can get in the way of leadership effectiveness by blinding people to their own limitations and causing them to overestimate their capabilities and performance.[9] In other words, it is not enough it be a resilient leader, one must also have integrity and care more about the welfare of their teams than their own personal success.

At no time in recent history has this need for resilience, rooted in compassion, been more evident than during these past three years living through a global pandemic. Our definition of

7. For example, McKinsey & Company is a consultancy firm whose purpose is to help companies increase resilience (https://www.mckinsey.com/).

8. Luthar et al., "Construct of Resilience."

9. Chamorro-Premuzic and Lusk, "Dark Side of Resilience."

"essential worker" has been both reinforced and redefined;[10] we've started questioning the meaning and methods for why, how, and for whom we work,[11] and for many women with children and people of color, especially, the economic effects of the pandemic have been particularly injurious.

Applying these lessons from COVID-19, we recognize that Christians in the workplace and in society generally, are not a monolithic group, and therefore, developing resilience through the practice of Sabbath will not look the same to everyone. That said, to respond to economic and social pressures in a manner that reflects core Christian beliefs, we propose a shared strategy of alignment with the will of God. Or as the apostle Paul put it, "Do not conform to the pattern of this world, but be transformed by the renewing of your mind. Then you will be able to test and approve what God's will is—his good, pleasing and perfect will" (Rom 12: 2 NIV).

The authors propose five areas where a more comprehensive understanding of Sabbath can assist believers to build resilience by reshaping their personal and professional identities in accord with God's will and purpose for their lives. They include the following:

1. Values—Sabbath as "reprioritization"

2. Time—Sabbath as "resistance"

3. Space/Place—Sabbath as "reimagination"

4. People—Sabbath as "renewal"

5. Faith—Sabbath as "redemption"

Sabbath as Reprioritization

Throughout the Gospels, Jesus explores several elements of the Decalogue, in new and expansive ways. He teaches that contempt for another person is tantamount to murder (Matt 5:21–22) and

10. Blau et al., "Essential and Frontline Workers."
11. Pew Research Center, "Majority of Workers."

that lust is synonymous with adultery (Matt 5:27–28). Similarly, he addresses other "sins of the heart," including a disordered love for material things:

> Do not store up for yourselves treasures on earth, where moths and vermin destroy, and where thieves break in and steal. But store up for yourselves treasures in heaven, where moths and vermin do not destroy, and where thieves do not break in and steal. For where your treasure is, there your heart will be also. . . . No one can serve two masters. Either you will hate the one and love the other, or you will be devoted to the one and despise the other. You cannot serve both God and money. (Matt 6:19–21, 24)

For Jesus, one's priorities and one's motives are as important as one's actions, and the purpose of the law was to correct, not punish. "The sabbath was made for man, not man for the sabbath," he tells the Pharisees (Mark 2:27), in defense of his practice of gleaning grain on the Sabbath, and then, "which is lawful on the Sabbath: to do good or to do evil, to save life or to kill?" (Mark 3:4), before healing a crippled man in the synagogue.

It was neither the crowd nor the religious elites whom Jesus sought to please but God the Father, whose being, nature, and character demand that we align our priorities with God's priorities and not the world's priorities. As the Teacher says,

> To humans belong the plans of the heart, but from the Lord comes the proper answer of the tongue. All a person's ways seem pure to them, but motives are weighted by the Lord. Commit to the Lord whatever you do, and he will establish your plans. (Prov. 16:1–3)

Richard Gaffin rightly notes that this sense of prioritization is at the heart of John Calvin's unique, and for some, controversial, understanding of Sabbath. The "inward reality" (*re ipsa interior*), corresponding to the "outward sign" (*signi externi*) given to Israel, is that

we must be wholly at rest that God may work in us; we
must yield our will; we must resign our heart; we must
give up all our fleshly desires . . . so that . . . we may repose in him (Heb. 4:9).[12]

Sabbath as reprioritization, then, begs the question, What is
the "purpose" of business generally? Are we to blindly accept the
so-called Friedman doctrine,[13] the belief that the maximization of
shareholder value is the sole purpose of business, or are we called
to consider alternatives, such as "stakeholder theory" and B-corp
models, etc.?

Answers to these questions are not tertiary but essential for
Christians who wish to align their personal experience of "meaning and purpose" at work and in business with biblical principles
and their own faith practice.

Sabbath as Resistance

As Prof. Walter Brueggemann notes in his book entitled *Sabbath
as Resistance*, the entire Decalogue is a denunciation not only of
the competing Gods of Israel's enslavers but the entire economic
system that subjugated them for the sake of Pharaoh's insatiable
appetite for material gain. There was clearly no time for Sabbath in
the Egyptian system, which forced the workers to produce bricks
without straw and to devote their entire lives to the building of
countless stores for the preservation of Pharaoh's excessive wealth,
military might, and religious hegemony (see Exod 5). As Brueggе-
mann puts it,

It requires no imagination to see that the Exodus memory and consequently the Sinai commandments are performed in a "no-Sabbath" environment. In that context
all levels of social power—gods, Pharaohs, supervisors,

12. Calvin, *Institutes*, 2.8.29.
13. Friedman, "Friedman Doctrine."

taskmasters, slaves—are uniformly caught up in and committed to the grind of endless production.[14]

Sadly, for many people today, that is a paradigm that rings true with their own experience in the workplace and no more so than in the global financial sector. A recent article in *Forbes* details the plight of junior analysts at investment firm Goldman Sachs complaining about one-hundred-hour work weeks, five hours of sleep per night, and general "workplace abuse," forcing the company to respond by promising to rigorously enforce its so-called "'Saturday rule'—which means that employees cannot work from 9 p.m. Friday to 9 a.m. Sunday except in certain circumstances."[15]

Of course, Goldman Sachs is not unique, nor is the financial sector the only place where workers find themselves under pressure to work excessive hours, respond to emails twenty-four seven and generally succumb to what some people have referred to as the tyranny of now—the overwhelming feeling that our employers, our colleagues, our culture—and even our friends and loved ones—demand instantaneous access to our minds, to our skills, and to our undivided attention, usually for the sake of their own ends and desires. Coconspirators in this effort are the purveyors of information technology, whose machines and algorithms numb us into a lemminglike existence and whose siren voices coax us deeper into a world where we lose both control and agency over our most precious commodity—our time.

The COVID-19 pandemic has exacerbated the "always at work" phenomenon, but history teaches us that the temptation to relinquish our thoughts, our time, and our talents to others has always been with us, and its dangers are well attested. No less a social commentator than Søren Kierkegaard warned his readers in the nineteenth century that it is an insidious thing to allow others to form our opinions for us, dictate our movements, define our values, and control our time. To follow the crowd is to relinquish

14. Brueggemann, *Sabbath as Resistance*, 5.
15. Kelly, "'100-Hour' Work Weeks," para. 1.

one's soul to the whims of fancy and the vagaries of popular culture. Or as Kierkegaard himself put it,

> The truth can neither be communicated nor be received without being as it were before the eyes of God, nor without God's help, nor without God being involved as the middle term, since he is the truth. It can therefore only be communicated by and received by "the single individual," which, for that matter, every single human being who lives could be: this is the determination of the truth in contrast to the abstract, the fantastical, impersonal, "the crowd."[16]

As we have enslaved ourselves by voluntarily succumbing to the pressures of "postmodern capitalism,"[17] we have inadvertently offered our bodies and our lives as living sacrifices, not to God, as demanded by the Scriptures (Rom 12:1), but to the cult of economic excess and devotion to Mammon (Mark 6:24).

One antidote to this heresy is the gift of Sabbath, Sabbath as resistance to the forces of both cult and culture that tempt us to displace the reign of God through the marginalization of God; these forces, if left unchallenged, ultimately distort our Christian values and contribute to the deterioration not only of society but of our own physical, emotional, and spiritual health.

Sabbath as Reimagination

Similarly, both technology and the constant pressure to perform in ways that are ever more stressful (and in many cases, unachievable) have conspired to deny us the God-given right to both personal and sacred spaces. The feeling of always being at work has blurred the lines between home and office, between labor and leisure, and made it harder for us to connect with God in both cathedrals of stone and nature.

16. Kierkegaard, "Crowd Is Untruth," para. 10.

17. Postmodern capitalism has been defined as an economic mutation of traditional capitalism that is "devoid of a moral compass and resistant, if not impervious to ethical constraint." See Barnes, *Redeeming Capitalism*, 18.

The Bible is replete with examples of God setting aside particular places for the purpose of spiritual delight and devotion, both public and private. From Mount Horeb to the Jordon Valley, from the temple in Jerusalem to the canopy of an evening sky, sacred space is presumed to be a source of both renewal and refreshment, not to mention an aide in the experience of transcendence. Jesus himself instructed his disciples to "go into your inner room and shut the door" when praying (Matt 6:6) and modelled the practice of solitude in prayer, even to the final days of his earthly life (Matt 26:36–46).

Sadly, as work has invaded our private spaces, it has also crowded out our sacred spaces. Home is no longer a sanctuary from the everyday stresses of economic activity but just another place where we "get things done." Social media is filled with videos of children "zoombombing" their parents' conference calls, demonstrating an innate sense of outrage over the intrusion of their privacy. Bedrooms that have been converted into workplaces have been shown to negatively affect both people's sleep patterns and their times of intimacy. Time with loved ones is intended to be sacred time, and the places where that time is spent are meant to be sacred space—not merely an extension of the workplace.

Lastly, we have lost the discipline of contemplation while seemingly taking the splendor and awe of God's majesty in our collective stride. Preferring to marvel at the wizardry of information technology, special effects, and virtual reality, we have neglected the wonder and extravagance of God's word, God's Creation, and God's love. This has brought us to a place of spiritual impoverishment, where we seek meaning and purpose in the trappings of material wealth instead of our place in the kingdom of God.

A broader understanding of Sabbath challenges the world's assumptions about wealth and worth and invites us to reimagine both our spirituality and our carnality—our relationships both with God and others. The comfort of a loving God who is always present has given way to an Orwellian intruder whose presence is always felt but never fully trusted, whose yoke is insufferable and whose benefits are temporal.

Is it possible that a sense spiritual of impoverishment is at the heart of increased incidents of anxiety and depression, especially as reported during the pandemic among young adults?[18] Is it also possible that this phenomenon has led to an increase in so-called "workplace spirituality"?[19] Perhaps, but one need look no further than the experience of the early church to see a model of work, worth, and wealth that reflects the wonder and awe of God's people living and working together for the good of the kingdom:

> And they devoted themselves to the apostles' teaching and the fellowship, to the breaking of bread and the prayers. And awe came upon every soul, and many wonders and signs were being done through the apostles. And all who believed were together and had all things in common. And they were selling their possessions and belongings and distributing the proceeds to all, as any had need. And day by day, attending the temple together and breaking bread in their homes, they received their food with glad and generous hearts, praising God and having favor with all the people. And the Lord added to their number day by day those who were being saved. (Acts 2:42–47)

Sabbath as reimagination gives us permission to look beyond the mundane, pedestrian nature of brute materialism to the wondrous, awe-inspiring nature of the divine; to reclaim our rightful place in the cosmos, our oneness with the Creator; and to reclaim the promise of eternal life in the very presence of God.

Sabbath as Renewal

It should be noted that the passage above from Acts 2 is neither a repudiation of capitalism nor an endorsement of socialism. Neither system represents the reality of economic activity in the ancient world. It is, however, a window into the economic culture of the early church. There is nothing "transactional" about the way

18. Ford et al., "Mental Health."
19. Vasconcelos, "Workplace Spirituality."

believers dealt with each other or the outside world. It is based upon a series of committed relationships, where both individuals and the community as a whole aligned the use of their material goods with their spiritual beliefs and practices.

Note how the passage begins by describing the church's devotion to both the teachings (*didache/διδαχή*) of the apostles and the fellowship (*koinonia/κοινωνία*) of believers. This was not an either-or situation. Christian teaching led to the integration of believer's lives because they saw themselves as "the body of Christ," which in turn led to the spiritual practices of Holy Communion and prayer. There was no possibility of a sacred/secular divide, nor was there any question as to the mutual benefits of living life together.[20] Furthermore, their devotion and their obedience led to a proliferation of "signs and wonders" and caused their number to grow by the day.

How different this model is from the reality of today's believers and nonbelievers alike, who have bought into the hyper-individualism of both religious practice and economic activity. Instead of merely lamenting the lack of mutuality and society's penchant for ethical egoism, the gift of Sabbath provides the opportunity for believers to renew the spirit of love and devotion that has defined not only the early church but every great movement of religious awakening in the history of Christendom.

Consider the example of the desert fathers (ca. third century), whose rejection of the world's values, devotion to prayer, meditation, recitation of Scripture, hospitality, and acts of mercy spawned similar monastic movements, from the Benedictines (ca. sixth century) to the Franciscans (ca. thirteenth century), to the Methodists (ca. eighteenth century) to the Taizé Community of today. Each one, a unique expression of the same phenomenon, but all defined by the depth and breadth of their dependence on God and their interdependence on one another.

This is not to suggest that only those who choose to live in monastic communities may live as genuine believers in the workplace. On the contrary, the values that they expressed are both

20. For a classic exploration of this concept, see Bonhoeffer's *Life Together*.

consistent with, and necessary for, a properly functioning free-market economy, and they are universally accessible. None other than Adam Smith famously wrote,

> No matter how selfish you think man is, it's obvious that there are some principles in his nature that give him an interest in the welfare of others, and make their happiness necessary to him, even if he gets nothing from it but the pleasure of seeing it.[21]

This, of course, includes one's economic activities. As Smith rightly notes,

> Political economy considered as a branch of the science of a statesman or legislator, proposes two distinct objects: first, to provide a plentiful revenue or subsistence for the people, or more properly to enable them to provide such a revenue or subsistence for themselves; and secondly, to supply the state or commonwealth with a revenue sufficient for the public services. It proposes to enrich both the people and the sovereign.[22]

For any person of goodwill, whether believer or nonbeliever, the purpose of work and economic activity, must surely be more than self-aggrandizement and the accumulation of personal wealth; it must first and foremost be driven by a genuine concern for the common good and love of neighbor.

Sabbath as renewal reaffirms all of God's covenants with his creation and presents us with a model that builds community on earth while anticipating the "new heaven and a new earth" to come (Rev 21–22).

Sabbath as Redemption

The early twentieth century American humorist and social critic Will Rogers famously quipped, "I've never met a self-made man who didn't worship his creator!" Perhaps a truer word has never

---

21. Smith, *Theory of Moral Sentiments*, 1.
22. Smith, *Wealth of Nations*, 429.

been spoken. The original sin of self-idolatry is alive and well, as is the cult of personality that attaches itself to so many "successful" women and men. Whether in business, politics, entertainment, sports, or the church, there are always people who allow themselves to be seduced by the adoration of others, until they start believing in their own perfection. When that happens, disaster is never far away. Sabbath, if properly observed, is an antidote to self-adulation, and a stepping stone on the road to redemption.

In the modern world, the pursuit of economic excellence has reduced almost every aspect of self-actualization to the relentless pursuit of self-gratification. A neo-Hedonistic cult has emerged that drives people to seek pleasure over purpose, matter over meaning, and stimulation over substance. It is a modern phenomenon, but there is nothing novel about it. It has existed for millennia, and no better example exists than the life of King Solomon.

The Bible teaches that Solomon "was greater in riches and wisdom than all the other kings of the earth. . . . The king made silver as common in Jerusalem as stones, and cedar as plentiful as sycamore-fig trees" (1 Kgs 10:23, 27 NIV). He ruled over Israel's golden age and was universally praised as a man of great wisdom. Despite his wealth, power, and prowess, he died a bitter and broken man, describing his own accomplishments as merely "chasing after wind" (Eccl 2:17 NIV). Soon after his death, his kingdom was divided, and his greatest achievement, the temple of Jerusalem, lay in ruins, even though God had warned him saying,

> If you or your descendants turn away from me and do not observe the commands and decrees I have given you and go off to serve other gods and worship them, then I will cut off Israel from the land . . . and will reject this temple. . . . [It] will become a heap of rubble. (1 Kgs 9:6–8)

Yet, Solomon did chase after other gods, and the one he worshipped most of all was probably himself. In the end, Solomon eschewed God's commands, ignored God's Sabbath, and lost faith in his Redeemer.

Centuries later Jesus himself would ask the question, "What good is it for someone to gain the whole world, yet forfeit their soul?" (Mark 8:36)—a question that every businessperson should ask themselves every day.

The Nobel Laureate, Bob Dylan, was correct when he penned the words to his famous song "You Gotta Serve Somebody." Everyone must eventually decide who they are going to serve and in whom they will put their faith. Choosing correctly is the first step on the road to redemption. Sabbath gives us the time and the space to re-prioritize and to reimagine the eternal meaning and purpose of our work. Sabbath gives us the power to resist the gods who would tempt us away from our Creator and renews us in our quest to make our work our worship (Rom 12:1–2). Sabbath prepares us for whatever the enemy may throw at us and whatever challenges may come at us. Sabbath may in fact be the ultimate form of resilience.

Further Reflection

The following chapters are further reflections on the themes discussed above. They represent the breadth and diversity of the fellows of the Mockler Center for Faith and Ethics in the Public Square. Some are deeply theological and/or philosophical, others are more practical and even whimsical. They are intended to help readers rethink their own understanding of Sabbath from a technical, biblical/theological, and pastoral perspective.

Bibliography

Barnes, Kenneth J. *Redeeming Capitalism*. Grand Rapids: Eerdmans, 2018.

Blau, Francine D., et al. "Essential and Frontline Workers in the COVID-19 Crisis (Updated)." Mar. 22, 2022. https://econofact.org/essential-and-frontline-workers-in-the-covid-19-crisis.

Bonhoeffer, Dietrich. *Life Together*. New York: Harper & Row, 1954.

Brueggemann, Walter. *Sabbath as Resistance*. Louisville: Westminster John Knox, 2017.

Calvin, John. *Institutes of the Christian Religion.* Translated by Henry Beveridge. Gaffin, Bristol: Mentor, 1998.

Chamorro-Premuzic, Tomas, and Derek Lusk. "The Dark Side of Resilience." *Harvard Business Review,* Apr. 16, 2017. https://hbr.org/2017/08/the-dark-side-of-resilience.

Ford, Tamsin, et al. "Mental Health of Children and Young People During Pandemic." *BMJ* 372.614 (2021). https://doi.org/10.1136/bmj.n614.

Friedman, Milton. "A Friedman Doctrine—The Social Responsibility of Business Is to Increase Its Profits." *New York Times Magazine,* Sept. 13, 1970.

Heschel, Abraham Joshua. *The Sabbath: Its Meaning for Modern Man.* New York: Farrar, Strauss & Giroux, 1951.

Kelly, Jack. "After Complaints Of '100-Hour' Workweeks, Goldman Sachs Is Allowing Bankers To Take Off On Saturdays." Apr. 14, 2022. https://www.forbes.com/sites/jackkelly/2021/03/23/after-complaints-of-100-hour-workweeks-goldman-sachs-is-allowing-bankers-to-take-off-on-saturdays/.

Kierkegaard, Søren. "The Crowd Is Untruth." 1847. Translated by Charles K. Bellinger. https://ccel.org/ccel/kierkegaard/untruth/untruth.i.html.

Luthar, Suniya S., et al. "The Construct of Resilience: A Critical Evaluation and Guidelines for Future Work." *Child Development* 71.3 (2000) 543–62. https://doi.org/10.1111/1467-8624.00164.

Parker, Kim, and Juliana Menasce Horowitz. "Majority of Workers Who Quit a Job in 2021 Cite Low Pay, No Opportunities for Advancement, Feeling Disrespected." Mar. 9, 2022. https://www.pewresearch.org/short-reads/2022/03/09/majority-of-workers-who-quit-a-job-in-2021-cite-low-pay-no-opportunities-for-advancement-feeling-disrespected/.

Ridenour, Autumn. *Sabbath Rest as Vocation: Aging Toward Death.* London: T&T Clark, 2018.

Smith, Adam. *An Inquiry into the Nature and Causes of the Wealth of Nations.* New York: MetaLibri, 2007.

———. *The Theory of Moral Sentiments.* Oxford, Bennett, 2008

Vasconcelos, Anselmo Ferreira. "Workplace Spirituality: Empirical Evidence Revisited." *Management Research Review* 41.7 (2018) 789–821. https://doi.org/10.1108/MRR-07-2017-0232.

Chapter Five

Sabbath as Reprioritization

AUTUMN ALCOTT RIDENOUR[1]

And God saw everything that he had made, and behold, it was very good. And there was evening and there was morning, the sixth day. Thus, the heavens and the earth were finished, and all the host of them. And on the seventh day God finished his work that he had done, and he rested on the seventh day from all his work that he had done. So, God blessed the seventh day and made it holy, because on it God rested from all his work that he had done in creation. —Gen 1:31—2:3[2]

Remember the Sabbath day, to keep it holy. Six days you shall labor, and do all your work, but the seventh day is a Sabbath to the Lord your God. On it you shall not do any work, you, or your son, or your daughter, your male servant, or your female servant, or your livestock, or the sojourner who is within your

1. For a more comprehensive discussion on Sabbath as belonging, see Ridenour, *Restlessness and Belonging*; and *Sabbath Rest as Vocation*.

2. All Scripture quotations in this chapter are taken from the ESV.

*gates. For in six days the Lord made heaven and earth, the
sea, and all that is in them, and rested on the seventh day.
Therefore, the Lord blessed the Sabbath day and made it holy.*
—Exod 20:8–11

*So then, there remains a Sabbath rest for the people of God, for
whoever has entered God's rest has also rested from his works
as God did from his. Let us therefore strive to enter that rest,
so that no one may fall by the same sort of disobedience.* —Heb
4:8–11

Introduction: Reprioritizing Sabbath

With digital technologies and online work demands increasing,
contemporary life has never felt more urgent or unending.[3] Increasingly, pastors, corporate leaders, and business ethicists are
returning to the power of Sabbath as a significant limit against the
tyranny of "now."[4] When work and communication exceed the
natural boundaries of time and space made available through new
technologies, the question pertaining to the meaning and purpose
of work, and thus the meaning and purpose of rest, are central.
Seeking theological wisdom on the subject involves a return to biblical and theological reflection from classic and modern sources,
including Jewish and Christian biblical interpretations, an analysis
of the role of Sabbath rest in the theology of St. Augustine, and
finally a reflection on the way rest circumscribes work along with
its implicit ethical values.[5] Turning to these sources helps ground
the meaning of work in the origin and end of its practice—that is,

3. Noble, *You are Not Your Own*; Crouch, *Life We're Looking For*.

4. Brueggemann, *Sabbath as Resistance*; see also Fadling, *Unhurried Life*;
Comer, *Ruthless Elimination of Hurry*; Scazzero, *Emotionally Healthy Spirituality*; and Crouch, *Techwise Family*.

5. While sleep, rest, and play might be considered universal needs, this
essay approaches rest informed by texts within the Jewish and Christian traditions. For arguments on the universal need for play, see Martha Nussbaum's
ten capabilities approach in *Women and Human Development* (80).

rest in God and fellowship with neighbor and creation. Through this overall analysis, I aim to synthesize some of the implications for Sabbath re-prioritization for the vocation of work, rest, and ordinary living.

The Sabbath Priority: Jewish and Christian Readings

The Hebrew concept of Shabbat or Sabbath reminds the Jewish and Christian traditions how God rests at the end of creation as well as commands rest as part of the law in the Mosaic covenant following Israel's liberation from Egypt. Rabbi Abraham Joshua Heschel reflects on the holiness of time personified through the Sabbath. Describing Sabbath as the "architecture of time," Heschel says,

> "And God blessed the seventh *day* and made it *holy*." There is no reference in the record of creation to any object in space that would be endowed with the quality of holiness. . . . On the Sabbath we try to become attuned to holiness in time. It is a day on which we are called upon to share in what is eternal in time, to turn from the results of creation to the mystery of creation; from the world of creation to the creation of the world.[6]

Turning attention from creation to the Creator of the world, Heschel reminds modern readers of the power in Sabbath and of the architecture of time written by eternity's design. Rather than finding holiness in an object of creation, instead, YHWH marks time with holiness and divine presence signifying moments filled with eternity.[7] Moreover, Heschel describes the Hebrew word *menuha* or rest as the day when the "universe was complete. . . .To the biblical mind *menuha* is the same as happiness and stillness, as peace and harmony."[8] In other words, Sabbath is the day of rest or completion, pointing to the completion of creation that results

---

6. Heschel, *Sabbath*, 8–10.
7. Heschel, *Sabbath*, 6.
8. Heschel, *Sabbath*, 22–23.

in worship. Sabbath is also a day of celebratory rest and reception shared with others. For this reason, Sabbath is a divine gift that shapes ordinary time, living, and work.

Similarly, New Testament Scholar Ben Witherington III also describes the significance of rest for the Christian faith. Witherington spends a significant portion of his work distinguishing between biblical interpretations by Seventh Day Adventist scholarship that argues for the significance of the literal seventh-day rest from eighth-day Sunday rest based on the resurrection of Jesus Christ. In the end Witherington departs from seventh-day Sabbath requirements based on his New Testament interpretation of the new covenant or new creation. However, he maintains a theology of rest that includes final rest in God based on Heb 3 and 4 and physical rest as creatures who are mortal and frail.[9] Drawing from eschatological interpretations of Isa 56:4–5, describing an everlasting covenant and Isa 66:23, in which the lion lays down with the lamb, Witherington highlights the teleological or eschatological dimension of rest for the redemptive future.[10]

Continuing his focus on rest, Witherington considers Heb 4 from the New Testament in connection with the LXX translations of Gen 2:2 and Ps 95, here underscoring "the idea of a day of rest . . . as yet another type on earth of God's ultimate rest—which means not so much an absence of activity, though that is a component, but the presence of joy, a sense of fulfillment and completion."[11] Practices of Jubilee anticipate a kind of fullness and provision made available through Sabbath rest. Here Witherington emphasizes the significance of divine presence and worship through the practice of rest and economic productivity that includes just limits. Paralleling the story of Joshua who enters Canaan, followers of Christ anticipate dwelling with God in their eternal home while practicing worshipful rest through ordinary living in the here and now.[12] New Testament theology emphasizes "the already/not

9. Witherington, *Rest of Life*.
10. Witherington, *Rest of Life*, 9.
11. Witherington, *Rest of Life*, 28.
12. Witherington, *Rest of Life*, 25–28.

yet" dimension in which Christians encounter divine presence as "partakers in Christ" while anticipating eschatological, heavenly fulfillment in eternal rest.[13]

Finally, Old Testament scholar Walter Brueggemann considers the significance of Sabbath in his recent volume *Sabbath as Resistance*. In this volume, Brueggemann highlights YHWH as distinctive from Pharaoh in the command to rest.[14] Unlike Pharaoh's restless command to build more bricks with endless work, YHWH commands rest while offering provision and the gift of restful limits. Rather than allowing work to serve as tyrant and master, the Creator commands rest for the good of creation through limits. In this way, YHWH is unlike other gods that require the endless maximization of profit as idol worship or commodity.[15] Likewise, Brueggemann emphasizes the significance of the fourth commandment as a hinge command between loving God in the first table and loving one's neighbor in the second table by standing guard against coveting in the tenth commandment.[16] For Brueggemann, the fourth commandment reminds individuals of their call to trust in God's provision, which guards against coveting or negative competition prohibited in the tenth commandment. Ultimately, Sabbath practice or focus on rest entails significant implications for work. But before considering these implications, I next consider the role of Augustine's theology and his teleological focus on Sabbath rest.

Augustine: Creatures Made for Sabbath Rest

Often quoted for his famous line, "You have made us for yourself, and our heart is restless until it rests in you," St. Augustine, bishop of Hippo (354–430 CE), establishes the foundational claim of what

13. Witherington, *Rest of Life*, 28.
14. Brueggemann, *Sabbath as Resistance*, xiii–xiv.
15. Brueggemann, *Sabbath as Resistance*, 86.
16. Brueggemann, *Sabbath as Resistance*.

it means to be human.[17] To be human is to be a creature. To be creaturely is to exist in relationship to the Creator. In this opening phrase, one can find the seeds of Augustine's overarching theology as one based on restlessness and love.[18] James K. A. Smith "recognizes that human beings are made by and for the Creator who is known in Jesus Christ," which constitutes a *design* claim with *teleological* implications in terms of our final purpose or end. From the outset, Augustine establishes our origin and end by which all meaning, purpose, and priorities will cohere for Christian living and thus, Christian ethics, including its implications for work and rest.

Augustine opens with a longing for rest and closes both his *Confessions* and *City of God* describing the end goal resulting in the "seventh day" or Sabbath rest. Closing the *Confessions*, he says, "The seventh day has no evening and has no ending. You sanctified it to abide everlastingly. After your 'very good' works, which you made while remaining yourself in repose, you 'rested the seventh day' (Gen 2.2–3). This utterance in your book foretells for us that after our works which, because they are your gift to us, and are very good, we also may rest in you for the Sabbath of eternal life."[19] In this way, Augustine book ends his theology by first longing for rest and then finding rest in the final Sabbath of God.

Likewise, Augustine structures his famous *City of God* describing two loves that built two cities—the first centered on love of God and the second centered on love of self with contempt for God. He concludes his detailed argument by describing Sabbath rest. Looking ahead to that day, he says,

> That will truly be the greatest of Sabbaths; a Sabbath that has no evening, the Sabbath that the Lord approved at the beginning of creation, where it says, "God rested on the seventh day from all his works, which he had been doing; and God blessed the seventh day and made it holy, because on that day he rested from all his works,

17. Augustine, *Confessions*, 3.
18. Smith, *You Are What You Love*, 8.
19. Augustine, *Confessions*, 304.

which God had begun to do." We ourselves shall become that seventh day, when we have been replenished and restored by his blessing and sanctification. There we shall have leisure to be still, and we shall see that he is God.[20]

We find fulfillment when entering the seventh day. Augustine builds on the creation narrative in which form and substance are created from nothing (*ex nihilo*) as well as filled through replenishment, restoration, and blessing unto sanctification. This blessing depends on divine providence, grace, and provision rather than ruthless competition or human effort alone.

Likewise, in Augustine's *On Genesis: A Refutation of the Manichees* he offers an allegorical interpretation of the seven days of creation, likening them to the seven stages of life and the seven epochs of history.[21] Building on Heb 3–4, Augustine recognizes eternal Sabbath is yet to come. In this way, Augustine's theology is purposeful. Moving toward our teleological goal of Sabbath rest, we are pilgrims living *in media res*, in the middle of things, in which we consider the role of work while living in this stage.

Known for his *Confessions*, an interior look at his own life journey *in media res*, Augustine seeks to understand his own motivations and dissatisfaction in his early life choices—whether relationships pursued through lust, petty theft involving infamous pears, or his successful career as a rhetor for Imperial Rome.[22] In each of these cases, he describes dissatisfaction, a sense of self-fragmentation, in which he analyzes the purpose (or teleological goal) behind his actions. At first, he concludes that he sought pleasure in lust, the "thrill" of getting away with theft, and success through his career.[23] Yet he also concludes that for each of these, he sought the approval of others. In terms of work and his successful speech writing for Imperial Rome, he experiences anxiety at the prospect of repeat performance cycles, much like an intoxicated beggar seeking the next hit. In this sense, he finds his work lacks

20. Augustine, *City of God*, 1090.
21. Augustine, *On Genesis*, 62–68.
22. Augustine, *Confessions*, 26–34, 96–98.
23. Augustine, *Confessions*, 27–28, 33–34, 96–98.

meaning or satisfaction tinged as it is with anxiety through its empty pursuits.[24]

Opening the *Confessions* with this sense of restlessness and anxiety, Augustine seeks the end of desire in some eternal good, the triune God, rather than temporal experiences, including his work and career. Diagnosing human motivation in terms of love or desire, Augustine describes his "order of love" in *On Christian Teaching*. Here he acknowledges a distinction between use and enjoy, as forms of love that either relate to an ultimate good (instrumental) or *for their own sake alone* (intrinsic). For Augustine, only one thing/*res*/reality can be loved for its own sake, the eternal Trinity—Father, Son, and Holy Spirit—as the beginning and end of all things.[25] As the origin and purpose to which all things orient or weigh, love of God remains *the priority* for Augustine's theology and ethics, with significant meaning for work and rest.

Augustine's order of love involves love for all created things as good, including work, insofar as these relate to the highest good or priority in eternal love of God. When objects or activities, such as work, are bereft of this love, they fall short of their transcendent goal. Serving God as the ultimate end orients and prioritizes all loves toward this end. But when creatures seek their final love or rest in created goods, worshipping the creature rather than the Creator, they turn in on themselves through disordered forms of love.[26]

Through disordered love, we too often exchange the creature for the Creator, or the "means for the ends," and find ourselves restless with temporal pursuits. As Jacques Ellul diagnoses, modern living does just this. It switches the means for the end. Thus, "the technological society," along with business and bureaucracy, are dominated by technique.[27] Technique focuses on the means (whether production, profit, or value propositions to be pursued) apart from formal and final goals. Eliminating design and

24. Augustine, *Confessions*.

25. Augustine, *On Christian Teaching*, 10.

26. Augustine, *Confessions*, 278. See also Rom 1:25.

27. Ellul, *Technological Society*.

teleology—or first and final causes that rest in the good of the Creator and creation—raises questions about identity and meaning. Pursuing maximum profit as the business model rather than the good achieved through some product, experience, or service implies that the means and ends are often switched. These habits can have negative impacts on multiple mainstream industries and institutions, whether medicine, education, communication (and public trust), technology, religion, or political service.[28] One can diagnose ways in which each of these industries are negatively impacted by the drive for profit that has altered many of these institutions' original goals.[29] In this sense, corporate interests that involve maximizing utility shape many of Western culture's values. Consuming goods is not simply confined to the marketplace but bleeds into the sacred spaces of human service and family life. Not surprisingly, perhaps, Andy Crouch diagnoses today's milieu as one enslaved to the empire of mammon.[30]

However, loving money is not a new problem. Paul exhorts believers that the love of money is the root of all kinds of evil while Jesus challenges the rich young ruler to give up his fortune for the sake of loving Christ (see 1 Tim 6:10; Mark 10:17–27). Augustine's order of love will account for ways our priorities are grossly misaligned, loving lower, temporal goods—whether gold, silver, or mammon—higher than God. Building on Augustine, the doctor of grace, in combination with Aristotle and scholastic theology, St. Thomas Aquinas considers disordered forms of love for mutable goods that depart from the final end of loving God, the immutable good. Among what are commonly known as the seven deadly sins, those particular vices that often pertain to work include greed, an inordinate love of money and possessions, and sloth, or "sadness about one's spiritual good, on account of

28. Postman, *Technopoly*; Postman, *Amusing Ourselves to Death*.

29. Postman, *Technopoly*; Postman, *Amusing Ourselves to Death*; Postman, *End of Education*, 25–36.

30. Crouch, *Life We're Looking For*, 75–78; Brueggemann, *Sabbath as Resistance*, 11.

the attendant bodily labor."[31] In other words, greed is associated with an insatiable desire for more while sloth, on the other hand, is commonly affiliated with laziness. However, William Mattison III claims sloth (*acedia*) may not be a vice for the lazy only but also for the successful, "type A" individuals who focus on work at the expense of their own spiritual development.[32] In other words, the crux of sloth is spiritual laziness, ignoring love of God as one's first priority (see Rev 2:4).

Still, we can conclude that all these vices, including sloth and greed, display disordered forms of love. For Augustine, virtue and vice are characteristics of love—in their fullest or most diminished forms. In this sense, work is a tangible good for creatures but becomes disordered when we love a lower good, whether work or profit, above the Creator. For this reason, I conclude with a section on the implications of pursuing Sabbath rest as our design and end in Christ, which offers meaning for both our center and circumference.

Relocating the Circumference in Work and the Center in Sabbath

Not unlike St. Augustine, twentieth-century theologian Karl Barth considers the meaning of Sabbath rest, describing God's own decision to rest from endless creation. In doing so, God treasures creation and delights in its goodness with "freedom, rest, and joy."[33] Just like God sets divine precedent for rest from creative work, so too should humans honor Sabbath rest as part of our created good and freedom before God through limitation.[34] Sabbath reminds individuals of the good in "being" rather than "doing" and in our created existence rather than productive accomplishments.[35] Barth

31. Aquinas, *Summa Theologica*, I-II.84.4.
32. Mattison, *Introducing Moral Theology*, 245.
33. Barth, *Church Dogmatics* III/1, 212–14.
34. Barth, *Church Dogmatics* III/1, 212–14.
35. Heschel, *Sabbath*, 3, 30.

establishes Sabbath as the "end, beginning, and interruption" before introducing the concept of work. Rhetorically, he asks if humanity can understand work apart from Sabbath, law apart from gospel. Like Augustine, Barth affirms Sabbath as part of our creative *design* and redemptive *telos*. In this way, Barth establishes the significance of the Sabbath command as well as describing some of its characteristics, including its social and celebratory aspects.[36]

Moreover, the Sabbath proves significant for "interrupting" or guiding individuals now living *in media res* between creation and redemption. Barth says, "In his week he will have to fix his eyes on one aim after another, yet not fall under the domination of any material or spiritual, individual or collective Mammon."[37] In other words, Sabbath provides the strong antidote to creation or idol worship, a temptation prevalent throughout the Old and New Testaments, as well as Augustine's order of love. Rethinking the purpose, meaning, quality, and goal of work finds its root in Sabbath. To live with radical dependence on God is countercultural and certainly counter "work" culture. Ordering work toward the Sabbath as its *telos* and goal reflects a different priority. In this way, work does not exist for profit or production (means) only. Like Augustine, Barth departs from work for its own sake and instead orients work for the sake of the kingdom, Sabbath, and glory of God.[38] Describing work's teleological orientation in Sabbath, Barth claims there is no independent meaning for work apart from God.

Furthermore, Barth emphasizes the distinction in the circumference and center for Christian living.[39] Noting work as circumference rather than center destabilizes the weight of work in a contemporary western culture prone to "hurry" and workaholism.[40] In this way, contemporary Sabbath practices include the beauty of "slowing down," and introduces the good found in methodical work as opposed to the frenetic pace of modern living.

36. Barth, *Church Dogmatics* III/4, 51.
37. Barth, *Church Dogmatics* III/4, 72.
38. Barth, *Church Dogmatics* III/4, 520–21.
39. Barth, *Church Dogmatics* III/4, 516.
40. Fadling, *Unhurried Life*; Noble, *You are Not Your Own*.

Guarding against hurried overwork, Alan Fadling says, "Overwork can end up like progress made on a treadmill. . . . There can be an ironic laziness about such work. The sheer quantity may be impressive, but quantity does not require as much effort from us as work that results in creativity, vitality or joy. In that sense, overwork can be lazy work."[41]

Turning to the value in methodical reflection and endurance changes the form and substance of work with implications for industry changes as seen in Victoria Sweet's *Slow Medicine: The Way to Healing*. Reclaiming time, empathy, and patient care over technology, efficiency, and productive work quotas, Sweet invokes what aligns with Sabbath reflection and meaning, drawing medicine back to its core purpose in healing presence.[42] This same principle might be applied to a host of industries—whether education, journalism, or politics—in order to retrieve these industries' origin and end.

In terms of criteria, Barth acknowledges that work involves creaturely, tangible elements like temporal provision and social cooperation. However, ordering work with this teleological grounding prevents us from turning it into an idol or misusing our neighbor through instrumental purposes without dignity. Work is for the good of society.[43] A Sabbath orientation offers meaning to work and helps guard against biblical injustice that exploits the neighbor or animal through mistreatment.[44] Sabbath places limits on labor and work that preserves the dignity and value of creatures as ends in themselves. As Norman Wirzba says, "Our work, if it is good, must line up sympathetically and harmoniously with God's."[45] With this goal, Wirzba says individuals should minimize work associated with a destructive toll and instead pursue work that includes justice for society and creation at large.[46] In this

41. Fadling, *Unhurried Life*, 47.
42. Sweet, *Slow Medicine*; Hauerwas, *Suffering Presence*, 81–82.
43. Barth, *Church Dogmatics* III/4, 542–43.
44. Barth, *Church Dogmatics*, 542.
45. Wirzba, *Living the Sabbath*, 95.
46. Wirzba, *Living the Sabbath*, 95.

sense, work and rest are necessarily social. This is best captured in Barth's acknowledgment, "Give *us* this day, *our* daily bread."[47] In this way, work informed by Sabbath provision seeks the good of self and neighbor in their mutually shared interest, as well as society, culture, and creation.

While work should include cooperation with others, it too often operates in isolation. Work directed at the Sabbath should guard against the modern temptation to work in isolation, recognizing that too often modern work is "worship" in its idolatrous form.[48] Instead, work should be oriented toward Sabbath where whole persons, body and soul, receive rest.[49] In this way, Barth and Augustine align well with Jewish/Christian biblical interpretations in their teleological focus on work for the sake of Sabbath rest, love, and worship of God. This final end involving worship of God begins and completes the work week by informing its meaning throughout the rest of our living in ordinary time. Thus, not only does Sabbath reframe and remind individuals "what we work toward," including our priorities and values that invoke divine presence, but it also provides the "training ground for the life of eternity, a preparation for the full reception and welcome of the presence of God."[50]

---

47. Barth, *Church Dogmatics* III/4, 536.

48. Barth, *Church Dogmatics* III/4, 536.Work as "worship" does not exclude Col 3:23–24, which says, "Whatever you do, do your work heartily, as for the Lord rather than for men, knowing that from the Lord you will receive the reward of the inheritance. It is the Lord Christ whom you serve" (NASB). In this sense, work is still a form of worship when committed to the honor and glory of God. Martin Luther will also describe secular work as a form of neighbor love. In this sense, work is not excluded from worship. However, work is not to become one's first love or idolatrous in form. This, unfortunately, is often the temptation in a post-industrial, tech-driven world.

49. Barth, *Church Dogmatics* III/4, 550, 53–54.

50. Wirzba, *Living the Sabbath*, 23–24.

Bibliography

Augustine. *City of God*. Translated by Henry Bettenson. London: Penguin, 1984.

———. *Confessions*. Translated by Henry Chadwick. Oxford: Oxford University Press, 1991.

———. *On Christian Teaching*. Translated by R. P. H. Green. Oxford: Oxford University Press, 1997.

———. *On Genesis*. Translated by Edmund Hill and Matthew O'Connell. Hyde Park, NY: New City, 2002.

Barth, Karl. *Church Dogmatics*. 4 vols. Edinburgh: T&T Clark, 1960.

Brueggemann, Walter. *Sabbath as Resistance: Saying No to the Culture of Now*. Louisville: Westminster John Knox, 2014.

Comer, John Mark. *The Ruthless Elimination of Hurry*. New York: WaterBrook, 2019.

Crouch, Andy. *The Life We're Looking For: Reclaiming Relationship in a Technological World*. New York: Convergent, 2022.

———. *The Techwise Family*. Grand Rapids: Baker, 2017.

Ellul, Jacques. *The Technological Society*. New York: Vintage, 1964.

Fadling, Alan. *An Unhurried Life: Following Jesus' Rhythms of Work and Rest*. Downers Grove, IL: IVP, 2013.

Hauerwas, Stanley. *Suffering Presence: Theological Reflections on Medicine, the Mentally Handicapped, and the Church*. Notre Dame: University of Notre Dame Press, 1986.

Heschel, Abraham Joshua. *The Sabbath: Its Meaning for Modern Man*. New York: Farrar, Straus & Giroux, 1951.

Mattison, William, III. *Introducing Moral Theology: True Happiness and the Virtues*. Grand Rapids: Brazos, 2008.

Noble, Alan. *You Are Not Your Own: Belonging to God in an Inhuman World*. Downers Grove, IL: IVP, 2021.

Nussbaum, Martha. *Women and Human Development*. Cambridge: Cambridge University Press, 2000.

Postman, Neil. *Amusing Ourselves to Death: Public Discourse in the Age of Show Business*. New York: Penguin, 1985.

———. *The End of Education: Redefining the Value of School*. New York: Vintage Books, 1995.

———. *Technopoly: The Surrender of Culture to Technology*. New York: Vintage, 1992.

Ridenour, Autumn Alcott. *Restlessness and Belonging: Augustinian Wisdom or the Digital Empire*. Waco, TX: Baylor University Press, forthcoming.

———. *Sabbath Rest as Vocation: Aging Toward Death*. London: T&T Clark, 2018.

Scazzero, Peter. *Emotionally Healthy Spirituality*. Grand Rapids: Zondervan, 2014.

Smith, James K. A. *You Are What You Love: The Spiritual Power of Habit*. Grand Rapids: Brazos, 2016.

Sweet, Victoria. *Slow Medicine: The Way to Healing*. New York: Riverhead, 2017.

Wirzba, Norman. *Living the Sabbath: Discovering the Rhythms of Rest and Delight*. Grand Rapids: Brazos, 2008.

Witherington, Ben, III. *The Rest of Life: Rest, Play, Eating, Studying, Sex from a Kingdom Perspective*. Grand Rapids: Eerdmans, 2012.

Chapter Six

Sabbath as Resistance

LARRY O. NATT GANTT, II

Time is money.[1]

THIS THREE-WORD APHORISM, ALTHOUGH stemming from an eighteenth-century essay by Benjamin Franklin, epitomizes how twenty-first-century Western culture views time. It is commoditized—intended for productivity, efficiency, maximization.

This fact is apparent in the legal profession perhaps more than in any other professional field in the United States. Lawyers' product is, in fact, their time. Lawyers do not produce widgets (the proverbial object in legal hypotheticals); clients pay lawyers for their expertise in providing legal advice and in solving legal problems. The dominant fee structure in the legal profession is the billable hour, in which lawyers charge clients for their time—usually in six-minute increments.[2] This fee structure still retains its

---

1. In his essay "Advice to a Young Tradesman," Benjamin Franklin wrote, "Remember that time is money." Franklin, "Advice to a Young Tradesman," 63.

2. Weaver, "Time We Rethink the Billable Hour." Although some lawyers

prominence despite numerous calls for change and numerous reports chronicling how the fee structure creates pressures that compromise lawyers' mental health and well-being.[3]

This fixation with commodifying time contrasts sharply with the biblical principle of Sabbath. Although this book richly recognizes the complexity of the concept of Sabbath, it is first and foremost about *time*:

> By the seventh day God had finished the work he had been doing; so on the seventh day he rested from all his work. Then God blessed the seventh day and made it holy, because on it he rested from all the work of creating that he had done. (Gen 2:2–3)[4]

> Remember the Sabbath day by keeping it holy. Six days you shall labor and do all your work, but the seventh day is a Sabbath to the Lord your God. On it you shall not do any work, neither you, nor your son or daughter, nor your male or female servant, nor your animals, nor any foreigner residing in your towns. For in six days the Lord made the heavens and the earth, the sea, and all that is in them, but he rested on the seventh day. Therefore the Lord blessed the Sabbath day and made it holy. (Exod 20:8–11)

This chapter will explore how our modern, Western conception of time—particularly in the professional world and in the legal profession specifically—has twisted the biblical conception of time. The chapter will also discuss how, once we apply a proper biblical conception of time to our lives, we can more fully appreciate the fullness and gift of the Sabbath.

---

do not charge clients based on their time, the ethos of the time billing and the billable hour is so pervasive in American legal culture that it affects even lawyers who bill time differently. See Kaveny, "Billable Hours in Ordinary Time."

3. See Smith, "Legal Industry's Mental Health Struggles Persist."

4. All Scripture quotations throughout this chapter are taken from the New International Version.

Modern Conception of Time

Before turning to a biblical perspective on time, it is worth exploring what sentiments "time" evokes in the modern secular mindset.
First, our modern conception of time is a relatively recent phenomenon. Although daily schedules and ordering daily life by the
clock were introduced to the West through the Benedictine mon-
asteries, concern about ordering individual life around specific
hours of the day was not important to individuals generally until
the dawn of the Industrial Revolution.[5] During the late nineteenth
century, the practice of "clock-watching" "turned into a veritable
obsession" as "railway timetables, time-stamped telegrams and
factory discipline all called for stricter conformity to the time of
the clock."[6] This growing preoccupation with time led to changes
in the ordering of individuals' lives. As Vanessa Ogle describes in
her book *The Global Transformation of Time: 1870–1950*,

> In the second half of the nineteenth century, workers and
> employers alike struggled over the meaning and division
> of social time, of work time and leisure, and the appro-
> priate proportion between them. Assigning certain divi-
> sions of time-specific tasks such as "work," "leisure," and
> "rest" gave rise to a heightened awareness for efficient
> time management among these collectives.[7]

The development of technology throughout the twentieth
century and into the twenty-first has reshaped the meaning and
apportionment of time, exacerbating our collective obsession with
time. In fact, particularly in this century, the ubiquity of technology—from hand-held devices containing everything we need to
artificial intelligence doing more and more of the things we need

5. Eviatar Zerubavel recounts how Benedictine monks observed a strict
regulation of time, with the day segmented into "hours" of prayer, sleep, and
work. See Zerubavel, "Benedictine Ethic and Modern Scheduling." See also
Bass, *Receiving the Day*, 26–27.

6. Johnston, "Marclay's Clock," para. 7. This fixation on time was only
made easier by the explosion in the number of personal watches by 1900. See
"Marclay's Clock," para. 6.

7. Ogle, *Global Transformation of Time*, 8.

to do is no doubt affecting our collective mood. Based on a survey it conducted in 2021, the Pew Research Center reported that 31 percent of US adults state that they go online "almost constantly," up from 21 percent in 2015.[8] Psychologists have, in turn, conducted recent studies finding that excessive smartphone usage is associated with sleep disorders and mental health problems.[9] This confluence of factors has even led to the coining of new maladies named "productivity shame" and its cousin "time anxiety." Productivity shame is the feeling that you never have done enough whereas, time anxiety is the feeling that you "never have enough time to meet your goals or that you are not maximizing the time you have."[10]

These mental health problems are particularly troubling in the legal profession. In 2017, the National Task Force on Lawyer Well-Being published its groundbreaking report *The Path to Lawyer Well-Being: Practical Recommendations for Positive Change*, which discussed the alarming rates of substance abuse and mental health problems among attorneys and law students.[11] The report recognized that one cause of this troubling data is how the frequent deadlines and heavy time demands of law practice often "rob lawyers of a sense of autonomy and control over their schedules."[12]

To diagnose the struggle more precisely in the legal profession—and see how those challenges relate to workers more

8. Perrin and Atske, "'Almost Constantly' Online," para. 1.

9. See, e.g., Reer et al., "Examining the Interplay."

10. Mackay, "Never Have Enough Time?," para 1.

11. National Task Force on Lawyer Well-Being, *Lawyer Well-Being*.

12. National Task Force on Lawyer Well-Being, *Lawyer Well-Being*, 16. The report adds, "Work cultures that constantly emphasize competitive, self-serving goals will continually trigger competitive, selfish behaviors that harm organizations and individual well-being" (33). See also Bergin and Jimmieson, "Australian Lawyer Well-Being," 427. The National Task Force Report spawned a well-being movement in the legal profession, which led to the development of the American Bar Association's Well-Being Pledge, signed by over 250 legal employers at the time of this writing, and to the formation of the Institute for Well-Being in Law, a nonprofit organization "dedicated to the betterment of the legal profession by focusing on a holistic approach to well-being." See Institute for Well-Being in Law, "How It All Began."

broadly—it is important to note that time is not just commodified in the profession; it is monetized. Attorneys in nearly all US law firms have a billable hourly rate and a minimum billable hourly requirement each year.[13] This double quantification (for instance, you are worth three hundred dollars an hour and you must bill two thousand hours per year) can result in attorneys' identity and worth being tied to—if not defined by—their work productivity. A 2022 survey of 3,400 legal professionals from law firms around the world, in fact, found that 60 percent of legal professionals identified billable-hour pressure as a top factor negatively affecting their psychological well-being.[14]

Personal stories are behind each data point and survey response, and one story of a lawyer suicide in 2018 galvanized perhaps like no other the calls for changes to improve attorney well-being in the legal profession. Gabe MacConnaill, a forty-two-year-old partner at Sidley Austin, a large law firm with offices around the world, committed suicide in September 2018 in the parking garage of the firm's downtown Los Angeles office. Less than one month later, MacConnaill's widow, Joanna Litt, shared her story in a poignant letter posted on Law.com, a well-known legal website. In the story, entitled "Big Law Killed My Husband: An Open Letter From a Sidley Partner's Widow," Litt shares how her husband felt tremendous pressure at his firm and "was doing the work of three people—and I think that's being generous." She explains how, after his death, she came across the concept of maladaptive perfectionism, which described her husband in many ways: "Simply put, he would rather die than live with the consequences of people thinking he was a failure. . . . I believe he died

---

13. The minimum billable-hour requirement can put tremendous time pressure on attorneys: "Nearly every law firm has a minimum billable hour requirement, typically 1,800 to 2,000 hours per year. This means a goal of approximately 7.7 billable hours per day—if you don't take a vacation, get sick or work weekends. Research shows that as much as two hours per workday is lost to non-billable tasks. So a lawyer needs to be at work 9.7 hours per day to bill 7.7." Vinaccia, "Capture Billable Time and Stress Less," para. 2.

14. Smith, "Pandemic Anxiety Wanes."

feeling overworked, inferior and undervalued."[15] As Litt's letter reflects, the well-being crisis in the legal profession stems from many factors, but researchers agree that time pressures serve as a foundational stressor for lawyers.[16]

Legal scholar and theologian M. Cathleen Kaveny perceptibly suggests that the billable hour pervasion affects lawyers' worldview on the conception of time in five foundational ways:

> First, it suggests that the value of a lawyer's time is entirely extrinsic (i.e., that it lies in achieving the purposes of the client and in making money for the firm); second, it teaches that time is a commodity with a readily identifiable monetary value; third, it presumes that all time is fungible; fourth, it suggests that lawyers live their lives in an endless, colorless present; and fifth, it contributes to the alienation and isolation experienced by many lawyers.[17]

Professor Kaveny's examination of the billable-hour culture provides an excellent springboard for considering time generally because her description reflects the larger secular mindset impacting professional settings across disciplines. Indeed, our modern worldview claims that our time is *ours* and that, regardless of whether we are a lawyer billing time to clients or any other individual seeking to schedule her time, we see it as a commodity we instrumentally "manage" or control to maximize our goals. We lean toward a myopic view of time that does not appreciate the social support we received from others that puts us in a position to be able to manage our time in the first place.[18]

---

15. Smith, "Pandemic Anxiety Wanes."

16. A comprehensive 423-page study published in 2022 on legal professionals in Canada extensively discusses the impact of the billable hour model on attorney wellness: "The pressure of billable hours on health, far from diminishing with experience, gradually drains professionals' resources while being associated with greater psychological distress, depressive symptoms, and feelings of burnout." Cadieux et. al., *Research Report*, 109.

17. Kaveny, "Billable Hours in Ordinary Time," 181.

18. Kaveny notes that a personal view of time overlooks, for instance, the time spent by teachers and mentors to enable the individual to get to the point

Moreover, because we experience life in and through time, how we view time impacts what we value.[19] The monetization of time in professional circles may cause us not to value (or value less) time spent on activities—from family gatherings to worship services to quiet times in nature—that do not advance this monetized agenda.[20] Indeed, our very nomenclature of "spending" time leads us to conceive of time narrowly as a monetized commodity to be valued for its utility.

Biblical Conception of Time

This modern secular conception of time contrasts sharply with the biblical conception. In describing this contrast, Professor Kaveny writes that from a Christian worldview,

> time is intrinsically rather than instrumentally valuable; it is not a commodity but a mystery; its moments are not fungible, but in significant ways unique; it is not an endless, colorless present, but a spiral punctuated by moments of decision. Finally, viewed in this theological and liturgical perspective, time does not lead to fragmentation and isolation but calls for personal integration and the nurturing of community.[21]

Each of these characteristics points to the fullness of the biblical conception.

First, although we often think of God's creation as things—such as water, land, animals, people—Genesis clearly indicates that God also created time as we know it.[22] In his book on Sabbath, which Autumn Alcott Ridenour also discusses in her chapter in this volume, Rabbi Abraham Joshua Heschel observes how religions generally focus on certain aspects of creation—namely,

of having discretion over the use of time. See Kaveny, "Billable Hours in Ordinary Time," 174, 185.

19. Kaveny, "Billable Hours in Ordinary Time," 175.

20. See Kaveny, "Billable Hours in Ordinary Time," 175.

21. Kaveny, "Billable Hours in Ordinary Time," 194.

22. Heschel, *Sabbath*, 3–5.

spaces and things—and not on time because they are easier to observe and manipulate. He responds that sacredness, however, is better found in time: "We must not forget that it is not a thing that lends significance to a moment; it is the moment that lends significance to things."[23]

Time therefore has inherent and intrinsic value as part of God's creation, like the value we more naturally see in created, living things.[24] Time is not valuable simply because we can accomplish something in it; its value is grounded in the fact that God acts in and through it to unfold his story of his relationship to humanity.[25] As Professor Kaveny writes, "To say that time is intrinsically valuable does not mean to say that human beings should not try to accomplish certain tasks, to achieve certain goals, in their allotted span of days. It does mean, however, that the value of those days cannot be encompassed entirely by the objectives we set for them."[26]

23. Heschel, *Sabbath*, 6.

24. "Inherent" and "intrinsic" have nearly identical meanings, but it is best to describe time's value with both adjectives and this chapter uses both. *Merriam-Webster* defines "inherent" as "involved in the constitution or essential character of something: belonging by nature or habit" (*Merriam-Webster*, s.v. "inherent," last updated March 6, 2025 https://www.merriam-webster.com/dictionary/inherent). It defines "intrinsic" in its first definition as "belonging to the essential nature or constitution of a thing," comparing it with "extrinsic" (*Merriam-Webster*, s.v. "intrinsic," last updated March 6, 2025 https://www.merriam-webster.com/dictionary/intrinsic). A more nuanced distinction implies that time's "inherent" value stems from its essential nature as part of God's creation whereas, time's "intrinsic" value stems from the fact that its value is internal and not based on extrinsic factors, such as what one accomplishes in it.

25. See Heschel, *Sabbath*, 6; see also Grudem, *Systematic Theology*, 172–73. "God can act in time *because* he is Lord of time. He uses it to display his glory. In fact, it is often God's good pleasure to fulfill his promises and carry out his works of redemption over a period of time so that we might more readily see his great wisdom, his patience, his faithfulness, his lordship over all events, and even his unchangeableness and eternity" (emphasis original).

26. Kaveny, "Billable Hours in Ordinary Time," 196.

Swiss theologian Hans Urs von Balthasar calls time "blessed spaciousness,"[27] and Scripture is replete with examples that call believers to appreciate that "spaciousness" as an opportunity to enjoy and bask in the presence of God, who "never leaves us" (Heb 13:5b). For instance, the Psalmists speak often of the virtue of "waiting" on the Lord.[28] Several different Hebrew words are translated as "wait" in these verses, including one as "wait silently" and others as "wait patiently."[29] Although a modern conception of time may have infected our concept of "waiting" as an opportunity to make the most of the time by doing something else while waiting, this biblical concept (again thinking about waiting silently or patiently) underscores that the time of waiting itself is intrinsically valuable. Indeed, many men and women in Scripture had to wait many years to see promises fulfilled—and God acted in and through these times of waiting to transform lives and shape character.[30] Historian Dorothy Bass points to the inherent value of time by beautifully stressing how the Bible teaches that "*time is a gift*." She adds, "When our emphasis on using time displaces our awareness of time as gift, we find that we are not so much using time as permitting time to use us."[31]

A corollary to this biblical principle that time is inherently and intrinsically valuable is that it is not commodifiable. The very practice of the billable hour represents the epitome of

<hr/>

27. Balthasar, *Theology of History*, 83–84.

28. E.g., Pss 25:3, 5, 21; 27:14; 33:20–22; 37:7, 9, 34; 39:7; 40:1; 62:5; 69:6; 130:5–6.

29. Qaw·wêh, hik·kə·tāh, wə·hit·hō·w·lêl are translated as "wait patiently"; dō·wm·mî is translated as "wait silently"; and qiw·wî·tî is sometimes translated as "wait patiently." See *Bible Hub*, Hebrew Interlinear Bible (https://biblehub.com/interlinear/).

30. As Vaneetha Rendall Risner writes concerning the twenty-five-year span between God's promise to Abraham and the birth of Isaac, "While Abraham was waiting, God was working. Molding his character. Teaching him patience. Building their friendship. It was in that 25-year wait that Abraham got to know God intimately. It was in those seemingly wasted years that God transformed him." Risner, "Unwelcome Gift," para. 10.

31. Bass, *Receiving the Day*, 2 (emphasis added).

commodification. "A commodity *per se* has no intrinsic value,"[32] and for many lawyers their time is valuable only when they can bill their clients for it.[33] Bass writes how time as commodity is exemplified in our datebooks and online calendars: "The flat pages of a datebook can become a template not simply for organizing time but also for visualizing what time is: a sequence of little boxes, each waiting to be filled."[34] Time thus has no value unless it is filled.

Such commodification flies in the face of God's perspective on time. Although God chooses to act through time, "God's own being does not have a succession of moments or any progress from one state to another. To God himself, all of his existence is somehow 'present' [and] God sees all time equally vividly."[35] Indeed, as the apostle Peter writes, "With the Lord a day is like a thousand years, and a thousand years are like a day" (2 Pet 3:8b).[36] We cannot fully comprehend this godly perspective on earth, but it must inform how we appreciate—and live out—each moment before us. We are called to grasp an eternal perspective of time in which we see each moment as part of a larger story—the details of every plot twist we do not know but the author, of which we do.

The billable hour model also teaches that time is fungible: that one hour worked on Monday morning has the same value as

32. Kaveny, "Billable Hours in Ordinary Time," 196. Kaveny further explains that a commodity's "worth is determined by how well it satisfies the pre-existing desires of consumers."

33. In fact, one technique law firms have used to incentivize certain behaviors for their lawyers, such as spending time in pro bono work, is to give those attorneys "billable-hour credit" for those activities as if they were working on matters for paying clients. See Hershenson, "Give Them Credit." Hershenson advocates law firms should also give billable-hour credit for hours spent on practices to enhance well-being and mental health.

34. Bass, *Receiving the Day*, 2. She adds that our modern conception of time has led to a false theology: "We come to believe that we, not God, are masters of time. We come to believe that our worth must be proved by the way we spend our hours and that our ultimate safety depends on our own good management" (Bass, *Receiving the Day*, 3).

35. Grudem, *Systematic Theology*, 169–70.

36. See also Ps 90:4: "A thousand years in your sight are like a day that has just gone by, or like a watch in the night."

one worked on Sunday morning.[37] The Bible, in contrast, teaches that "each moment is understood to carry a certain uniqueness."[38] On this point, Rabbi Heschel writes, "Unlike the space-minded man to whom time is unvaried, iterative, homogeneous, to whom all hours are alike, qualitiless, empty shells, the Bible sees the diversified character of time. There are no two hours alike. Every hour is unique and the only one given at the moment, elusive and endlessly precious."[39] Old Testament law, for instance, is replete with specifications for feasts and traditions that are intended to be carried out during the year *at certain times*, tied to the natural order of the seasons.[40] The liturgical calendar of current church traditions similarly progresses through the year with periods *at certain times* designed to reflect important moments in salvation history.[41] Christians therefore are encouraged to appreciate each moment as unique, which has particular application as one considers the special import of Sabbath in this rhythm, as discussed below.

Finally, a capstone to these principles outlining the biblical conception of time is that time is more than a "vocational treadmill," with no larger purpose other than professional productivity, however defined.[42] The biblical narrative shows us instead that each moment we enjoy is part of a larger purpose. God's story has a point: "It is teleologically ordered toward a goal—the full instantiation of the kingdom of God."[43] In this ordering, time is "not an

37. Kaveny, "Billable Hours in Ordinary Time," 188.
38. Kaveny, "Billable Hours in Ordinary Time," 200.
39. Heschel, *Sabbath*, 8.
40. See, e.g., Lev 23, which describes the Sabbath along with seven feasts: the Feast of Passover, the Feast of Unleavened Bread, the Feast of Firstfruits, the Feast of the Harvest (or Weeks), the Feast of Trumpets, the Day of Atonement, and the Feast of Tabernacles.
41. Kaveny, "Billable Hours in Ordinary Time," 201. Here, Kaveny notes how the liturgical year moves from Advent and Christmas to Easter to Pentecost and ends in, some traditions, with the feast of Christ the King. For a discussion of liturgical calendars generally, see Jones et al., *Study of Liturgy*.
42. Kaveny, "Billable Hours in Ordinary Time," 204.
43. Kaveny, "Billable Hours in Ordinary Time," 207. As the theologian and

endless, purposeless extension but a spiral that gathers in the past even as it moves toward an eschatological future that is best evoked by the metaphor of the kingdom of God."[44]

Relevance to Sabbath

These observations about time generally have clear implications for our specific conception of Sabbath. Perhaps most notably, Sabbath is not an esoteric construct but rather is particularly situated in time. Because time is not fungible and each moment is a gift of God for a special purpose, Christians should seek to keep the Sabbath as an act of gratitude and worship and in recognition that it situates them in the mystical rhythms of life ordered by the teleological purpose of reflecting the kingdom of God. Biblical references to Sabbath make clear that the Sabbath is *holy* and therefore believers' devotion to Sabbath should reflect this sacredness.[45]

That honoring the Sabbath is important begs the question of what interval of time constitutes the Sabbath. Contemporary discussions of Sabbath-keeping sometimes focus on encouraging believers to dedicate particular time to God but shy away from suggesting they designate a full "day" to Sabbath. The biblical references noted above and others, however, plainly describe Sabbath as a Sabbath "day"; and the same Hebrew word is used in Gen 1 to describe the days of creation as is used in Gen 2 to describe the Sabbath day and in Exod 20 to describe the fourth commandment.[46]

Moreover, that the day as an interval of time might have special meaning when considering Sabbath resonates with many

monk Lluis Duch writes, time devoted to Christian sacraments, for instance, is not "mere 'distraction,' 'boredom' or a pause in the febrile activity of man dedicated to ever-greater productivity." Duch, "Experience and Symbolism of Time," 26.

44. Kaveny, "Billable Hours in Ordinary Time," 209.

45. Erickson, *Christian Theology*, 702.

46. Scriptures uses the same word יוֹם (yō·wm) in all of these references in Gen 1 and 2 and in the reference in the Ten Commandments in Exod 20:11. See *Bible Hub*, s.v. "yō·wm," https://biblehub.com/hebrew/yom_3117.htm.

biblical passages that highlight the day as a particularly meaningful cycle in the overall trajectory of time. As Dorothy Bass writes,

> In the creation hymn that begins the Jewish and Christian scriptures, the first act of God is to create light and, seeing that it is good, to separate it from darkness. This is the beginning of time, which from that moment on bears the forms of Day and Night, as God's first gifts are repeated again and again (Genesis 1:1–5). . . . Throughout the continuing saga of God's people, it is on these that God will hang blessing after blessing. Even when desolate and far from home, prophets declare that God's mercies are "new every morning" (Lamentations 3:23).[47]

The expansion of technology—from the ubiquity of electric light to the constant of internet access—has enabled us to divorce our conception and experience of time from this daily rhythm. There is no doubt, however, that we cannot control the rising and setting of the sun. The duration of the day is "given by a movement beyond our human power to control."[48]

As one example of the import of each day, Bass points to the biblical account of God's provision of manna to the Israelites after their exodus from Egypt. Manna would keep for only one day, except the Sabbath day, such that on the sixth day, the Israelites could safely gather two days' supply.[49] God's provision underscores the import of daily rhythm—that each day is a new opportunity to trust and to worship—and the rhythm of the Sabbath day in particular. This focus on the day throughout Scripture diminishes the spiritual significance of minutes and hours, given that these are human constructs that were not even agreed upon until relatively recently in human history.[50] Keeping Sabbath minutes or hours throughout the week implies that Sabbath is determined by the

---

47. Bass, *Receiving the Day*, 4; see also Matt 6:34: "Therefore do not worry about tomorrow, for tomorrow will worry about itself. Each day has enough trouble of its own."

48. Bass, *Receiving the Day*, 16.

49. Bass, *Receiving the Day*, 13.

50. Bass, *Receiving the Day*, 16.

clock, not by God, and it trivializes the significance of keeping the Sabbath *day.*

In addition, the rhythm of six and then one is a pattern we see in other biblical practices related to sabbatical principles.[51] Exodus 23:10–11 and Lev 25:1–7 designate a Sabbath year for farmland, vineyards, and olive groves in which every seven years this land is to lie unplowed and unused. Exodus 21:2 and Deut 15:12–18 provide that the servitude of Hebrew servants was limited to six years, as in the seventh year they are to "go free." Deuteronomy 15:12–18 outlines the Sabbath year for canceling debts, a year in which Israelites are instructed to cancel any loan they made to fellow Israelites. Finally, Lev 25:8–55 details instructions for the Year of Jubilee, the year after every seventh Sabbath year, including the instruction to return land purchased in the interim years to the original landowners. These sabbatical rhythms in other contexts highlight that the Sabbath rest, as one day in every seven, is a mystical pattern God designed for humanity.[52] As Professor Ridenour notes in her chapter, Rabbi Heschel calls Sabbath a part of God's "architecture of time,"[53] and humankind is therefore not at liberty to change its structure.[54]

Keeping the Sabbath

Surveying the many suggested approaches on how Christians should specifically honor the Sabbath through their time is beyond the scope of this chapter. Certain general observations, however,

---

51. Recognizing this import of Deut 15, Walter Brueggemann calls believers to "seven" our lives in which we see the relevance of sabbatical principles to all areas of life. Brueggemann, *Sabbath as Resistance*, 43–44.

52. Hayford, *Bible Handbook*, 747. "The Sabbath is a means by which man's living pattern imitates God's manifest pattern for life on this planet."

53. Heschel, *Sabbath*, 8.

54. Jesus condemned the pharisaical regulations that missed the deep spiritual significance of the Sabbath, but he did not condemn this structure. See, e.g., Mark 2:23–28; see also Hayford, *Bible Handbook*, 747.

flow directly from the discussion here of the biblical conception of time.

First, if time is inherently and intrinsically valuable as a gift, devoting time to the Sabbath is not about giving God what is ours; it is about receiving from God what is his. Sabbath-keeping allows us to recognize—through whatever specific practices one adopts—that all time is from God.[55] Indeed, that time is a gift reflects the broader notion that, as God's creation, everything humanity has is derived from God.[56] *Stewardship* as a biblical principle is not just about physical things; it is also about time.[57] Sabbath-keeping is thus part of our overall act of stewardship in which we carefully and responsibly take care of those things—including time—that are "entrusted" to us.[58]

Second, the modern tyranny of time can be avoided by underscoring that time is a gift from God and that, because all his creation is good, its very nature is not tyrannical and is intended as a blessing.[59] The Sabbath commandment emphasized to the Israelites God's goodness and provision in direct contrast to their tyrannical enslavement in Egypt, where their time was valued based only on their productivity.[60] Jesus' teaching that the Sabbath was "made for man" reflects this freedom inherent in Sabbath (see Mark 23:27). We therefore should not return to a servile mindset and be stressed or anxious as we discern how best to steward the

55. Fretheim, *Exodus*, 229. "People are not to live as if all time were their own, to do with as they please. The God of all time retains the right to determine how one day shall or shall not be used."

56. Erickson, *Christian Theology*, 511. "Since we would not be alive but for God, everything we have and are derives from him."

57. Erickson, *Christian Theology*, 511. Seeing stewardship as applicable to time underscores the similar foundational principles behind tithing financial income and Sabbath-keeping. See Jewell, "Sabbath."

58. *Merriam-Webster* defines "stewardship" as "the careful and responsible management of something entrusted to one's care." *Merriam-Webster*, s.v. "stewardship," last updated March 6, 2025, https://www.merriam-webster.com/dictionary/stewardship.

59. See Gen. 1:31: "God saw all that he had made, and it was very good. And there was evening, and there was morning—the sixth day."

60. See Brueggemann, *Sabbath*, 21.

gift of time; rather, we should view that discernment process as an opportunity to enjoy the "blessed spaciousness" of time in order to honor God and serve others.[61]

Third, the principle of stewarding time might also create anxiety in some Christians as they strive to maximize their time for God. This form of "time anxiety" may be well-intentioned in that they are seeking to follow Col 3:23 in doing everything "with all your heart, as working for the Lord." This anxiety can especially arise in many lawyers and others who already struggle with a distorted view of time as solely valuable instrumentally, based on what can be accomplished in it. Sabbath-keeping, however, is not measured by how "productive" we are—even in honoring God. Sabbath is by its very nature reflective in that it comes *after* six days of work. Sabbath "frees us from the need for productivity and allows us instead to enjoy what has already been made."[62] It is an antidote to the "anxiety system" that pervades our workplaces, including in the field of law, and our entire social system.[63]

We live in a world where busyness often signals importance, and we face the temptation to fill up our Sabbath time with nonwork-related accomplishments.[64] Returning to the origin of Sabbath reminds us that God did not turn from creating to other godly tasks on the Sabbath day; he *rested*.[65] Resting on the Sabbath

61. Peter encouraged the early church to use their spiritual gifts to serve others. See 1 Pet. 4:10: "Each of you should use whatever gift you have received to serve others, as faithful stewards of God's grace in its various forms." Similarly, we should use our gift of time to serve others.

62. Ryken, *Work and Leisure in Christian Perspective*, 183. As noted above, the Sabbath rhythm of work and rest is an example of the larger rhythm of work and rest in the annual feasts of the Old Testament. See Ryken, *Work and Leisure*, 185.

63. See Brueggemann, *Sabbath*, 31–32.

64. As Justin Whitmel Earley observes, "It used to be that the upper class showed off their status by displaying their lives of leisure. Now we do it by conspicuously displaying our lives of constant busyness. The more important you are, the more in demand your time is, so nobody who is anybody has time for enough sleep." Earley, *Common Rule*, 145.

65. As Walter Brueggemann recognizes, God's rest on the Sabbath was not from "exhaustion but in serenity and peace," as he reflected on his creation.

reminds us, in a completely countercultural way, that our identity is not based on our productivity or accomplishments but on our created status as image bearers of the King.[66] In fact, time to rest on Sabbath protects us from the tyranny of time and helps us recognize that we cannot "get it all done" and that our ultimate trust should not be in our own abilities but in our trust and reliance on God.[67]

Personality research on lawyers finds that lawyers generally are highly skeptical; they "like to be in control" and do not like others "telling them what to do."[68] The tragic story of Gabe MacConnaill exemplifies how many lawyers also struggle with perfectionistic tendencies by which they establish unrealistic expectations of achievement and are highly self-critical if they fail to meet those expectations.[69] This message of trust is thus especially challenging for those in the legal profession.

This same message, however, also strikes a deeper chord that resonates with lawyers—and with us all. Understanding and applying Sabbath living profoundly impacts our entire worldview. We not only see time as a gift but, we also "live by gift" in which we more fully appreciate God's grace.[70] Karl Barth writes, "The commandment of the sabbath day explains all the other commandments. For by requiring human beings to refrain from their own work, it explains that the commanding God, who has enabled and

---

Brueggemann, *Genesis*, 35.

66. See Brueggemann, *Sabbath*, 21. "Resting" on the Sabbath does not mean doing nothing; it means doing restful things, such as worship, prayer, spending time in nature, and spending time with those we love. See Earley, *Common Rule*, 149. What individuals see as restful can change depending on how they spend their time during the other parts of the week. Earley, *Common Rule*, 150–51.

67. Early reflects on how observing the Sabbath "helps me see how small I am." Earley, *Common Rule*, 152–53.

68. Larry Richard, quoted in Mack and Bloom, "Lawyers As Leaders," para. 4.

69. See Moraites, "Perfectionism."

70. See Brueggemann, *Sabbath*, 21. See also Jas 1:17: "Every good and perfect gift is from above, coming down from the Father of the heavenly lights, who does not change like shifting shadows."

commissioned human beings for [that] work, is the one who is gracious to them in Jesus Christ."[71] In sum, observing the Sabbath points us to the core truth of the gospel: our salvation is based not on what we do but on what God has done for us through the death and resurrection of Jesus Christ.

Bibliography

Balthasar, Hans Urs von. *A Theology of History*. New York: Sheed and Ward, 1963.

Barth, Karl. *Insights: Karl Barth's Reflections on the Life of Faith*. Louisville: Westminster John Knox Press, 2009.

Bass, Dorothy C. *Receiving the Day: Christian Practices for Opening the Gift of Time*. San Francisco: Jossey-Bass, 2000.

Bergin, Adele J., and Nerina L. Jimmieson. "Australian Lawyer Well-Being: Workplace Demands, Resources and the Impact of Time-Billing Targets." *Psychiatry, Psychology and Law* 21.3 (2014) 427–41.

Brueggemann, Walter. *Genesis: Interpretation: A Bible Commentary for Teaching and Preaching*. Atlanta: John Knox Press, 1982.

————. *Sabbath as Resistance: Saying No to the Culture of Now*. Louisville: Westminster John Knox Press, 2017.

Buchanan, Bree, et al. *The Path to Lawyer Well-Being: Practical Recommendations for Positive Change*. National Task Force on Lawyer Well-Being. 2017. https://lawyerwellbeing.net/wp-content/uploads/2017/11/Lawyer-Wellbeing-Report.pdf.

Cadieux, Nathalie, et. al. *Research report (Final Version): Towards a Healthy and Sustainable Practice of Law in Canada: National Study on the Health and Wellness Determinants of Legal Professionals in Canada, Phase I (2020–2022)*. Université de Sherbrooke, Business School. 2022. https://flsc.ca/wp-content/uploads/2022/12/EN_Report_Cadieux-et-al_Universite-de-Sherbrooke_FINAL.pdf.

Duch, Lluis. "The Experience and Symbolism of Time." In *The Times of Celebration*, edited by David Power and Marcus Lefebure, 22–28. Concilium 142. New York: Seabury, 1981.

Earley, Justin Whitmel. *The Common Rule: Habits of Purpose for an Age of Distraction*. Downers Grove, IL: InterVarsity, 2019.

Erickson, Millard J. *Christian Theology*. 2nd ed. Grand Rapids: Baker, 1998.

Franklin, Benjamin. "Advice to a Young Tradesman." In *Benjamin Franklin and Jonathan Edwards: Selections From Their Writings*, edited by Carl Van Doren, 63–64. New York: Scribner's Sons, 1920.

71. Barth, *Insights*, 102.

Fretheim, Terence E. *Exodus*. Interpretation. Louisville: Westminster John Knox Press, 1991.

Grudem, Wayne. *Systematic Theology: An Introduction to Biblical Doctrine*. Grand Rapids: Zondervan, 1994.

Hayford, Jack W., ed. *Hayford's Bible Handbook*. Nashville: Thomas Nelson, 1995.

Hershenson, Emily Harten. "Give Them Credit: Attorneys, Mental Health, and the Billable Hour." Law.com. July 1, 2022. https://www.law.com/2022/07/01/give-them-credit-attorneys-mental-health-and-the-billable-hour/.

Heschel, Abraham Joshua. *The Sabbath: Its Meaning for Modern Man*. New York: Farrar, Straus & Giroux, 2005.

Institute for Well-Being in Law. "How It All Began: The Evolution from the National Task Force to the Institute for Well-Being in Law." https://lawyerwellbeing.net/how-it-all-began/.

Jewell, Brian. "The Sabbath: A Tithe of Your Time?" *God, Money & Me*, June 18, 2013. https://www.godmoneyme.com/2013/06/18/the-sabbath-a-tithe-of-your-time/.

Johnston, Jean-Michel. "Marclay's Clock: 24-Hour Installation Highlights a Modern Obsession with Time." *The Conversation*, Apr. 11, 2019. https://theconversation.com/marclays-clock-24-hour-installation-highlights-a-modern-obsession-with-time-115183.

Jones, Cheslyn, et al., eds. *The Study of Liturgy*. New York: Oxford University Press, 1992.

Kaveny, M. Cathleen. "Billable Hours in Ordinary Time: A Theological Critique of the Instrumentalization of Time in Professional Life." *Loyola University Chicago Law Journal* 33.1 (2002) 173–220.

Mack, Olga V., and Katia Bloom. "Lawyers As Leaders: Is Your Personality Too Legal?" *Above the Law*, June 12, 2017. https://abovethelaw.com/2017/06/lawyers-as-leaders-is-your-personality-too-legal/.

Mackay, Jory. "Feel Like You Never Have Enough Time? Try These 5 Ways to Cope with the Anxiety." *Fast Company*, Nov. 29, 2020. https://www.fastcompany.com/90579824/feel-like-you-never-have-enough-time-try-these-5-ways-to-cope-with-the-anxiety.

Moraites, Robynn. "Perfectionism—Part 2: Maladaptive Perfectionism." *North Carolina Lawyer Assistance Program*, Nov. 22, 2022. https://www.nclap.org/perfectionism-part-2-maladaptive-perfectionism/.

Ogle, Vanessa. *The Global Transformation of Time: 1870–1950*. Cambridge: Harvard University Press, 2015.

Perrin, Andrew, and Sara Atske. "About Three-in-Ten U.S. Adults Say They Are 'Almost Constantly' Online." Pew Research Center. Mar. 26, 2021. https://www.pewresearch.org/fact-tank/2021/03/26/about-three-in-ten-u-s-adults-say-they-are-almost-constantly-online/.

Reer, Felix, et al. "Examining the Interplay of Smartphone Use Disorder, Mental Health, and Physical Symptoms." *Frontiers in Public Health* 10.834835 (2022) 1–10. https://doi.org/10.3389/fpubh.2022.834835.

Risner, Vaneetha Rendall. "The Unwelcome Gift of Waiting." Desiring God. June 15, 2016. https://www.desiringgod.org/articles/the-unwelcome-gift-of-waiting.

Ryken, Leland. *Work and Leisure in Christian Perspective.* Eugene, OR: Wipf & Stock, 1987.

Smith, Patrick. "Pandemic Anxiety Wanes, but Legal Industry's Mental Health Struggles Persist." Law.com. May 10, 2022. https://www.law.com/2022/05/10/pandemic-anxiety-wanes-but-legal-industrys-mental-health-struggles-persist/.

Vinaccia, Jacqueline. "Capture More Billable Time and Stress Less." Last updated Dec. 9, 2024. https://www.attorneyatwork.com/billable-time-stress-less/.

Weaver, Eleanor. "It's About Time We Rethink the Billable Hour." *Lawyer Monthly*, June 7, 2021. https://www.lawyer-monthly.com/2021/06/its-about-time-we-rethink-the-billable-hour/.

Zerubavel, Eviatar. "The Benedictine Ethic and the Modern Spirit of Scheduling: On Schedules and Social Organization." *Sociological Inquiry* 50.2 (Apr. 1980) 157–69. https://doi.org/10.1111/j.1475-682X.1980.tb00383.x.

Chapter Seven

Sabbath as Reimagination

KARA MARTIN

Introduction: Sabbath as Lothlórien

FRODO AND HIS COMPANIONS—THE Fellowship of the Ring—set out on a dangerous journey, seeking to destroy the one ring of power in the fires of Mount Doom, in the heart of enemy territory. This is the story arc for J. R. R. Tolkien's *Lord of the Rings*, a classic both of literature and more recently film.

What has fascinated many writers, including me, is the rhythm inherent in Tolkien's work. In a review of Ursula Le Guin's essay on Tolkien, Merle Rubin says Le Guin "shows how Tolkien alternates scenes of lightness and darkness, warmth and cold, difficulty and reprieve, travel and rest to create an ongoing sense of movement and life."[1]

What Le Guin captures is the rhythm that is not just built into the narrative but flows out of Tolkien's Catholic faith.[2] These

1. Rubin, "Mind Falls into Rhythm," 3.
2. "J. R. R. Tolkien, the author of *The Lord of the Rings*, called his book 'a

"alternate scenes of . . . travel and rest" are the rhythms of work and Sabbath. It is these moments of rest in Tolkien's work that particularly speak to me. In these moments there are three things that go on: a deep sense of place, a space created for contemplation, and the opportunity for imagination.

In just the first book of the *Lord of the Rings* trilogy, there are three times when Frodo and his companions get to rest from the travails of their journey: at the enigmatic Tom Bombadil's (omitted from the movie), at Elrond's home Rivendell, and with Lady Galadriel at Lothlórien.[3] This chapter will focus on the third rest to introduce the three themes mentioned and then explore the themes more fully in biblical and theological context, and with reference to other writers who have engaged with Sabbath, including the poets Wendell Berry and David Whyte.

Sabbath in Lothlórien

When Frodo and his companions stumble into Lothlórien, they are weary and fearful, pursued by orcs, and mourning the loss of their guide and protector, Gandalf the Grey. After a time of testing by sentinels, they are welcomed into the community of the woodland elves and eventually meet the rulers of that realm, Galadriel and Celeborn.

> Immediately, Frodo has a sense of the importance of this place: As soon as he set foot upon the far bank of Silverlode a strange feeling had come upon him. . . . It seemed to him he had stepped over a bridge of time into a corner of the Elder Days and was now walking in a world that was no more.[4]

---

fundamentally religious and Catholic work.' He was a devout Catholic himself, and he regarded the Gospel as the ultimate story." Pieters, "Christian Symbolism," para. 1.

3. Tolkien, *Lord of the Rings*, 138, 235, 351.

4. Tolkien, *Lord of the Rings*, 368.

All the company are struck by the beauty of the place: the colors and the fragrance. As one sentence captures it: "In winter here no heart could mourn for summer or for spring."[5]

This elven realm is the centre of elvendom on Middle Earth, as Aragorn explains, and has been an outpost of good holding back the evil of Sauron.[6] The wonder of the place becomes more obvious to them when it is time to leave. "Their hearts were heavy; for it was a fair place, and it had become like home to them."[7]

The importance of being in this place outweighs the importance of time. In fact, the passage of time had no meaning. After they emerge, Sam is confused at the shape of the moon, because by his calculation they were in Lothlórien for just three nights. However, the reality is that they were there far longer. Aragorn tells Sam that, "There time flowed swiftly by us. . . . The old moon passed and a new moon waxed and waned in the world outside, while we tarried there."[8]

Within Lothlórien, the companions experience rest, yes, but something much deeper than mere physical rest—the opportunity for contemplation. They get the chance to relive their journey and properly lament their lost companion Gandalf. "As they were healed of hurt and weariness of body the grief of their loss grew more keen."[9] The elves and Frodo sing songs of sorrow.

After this period of contemplation, they have the opportunity to consider the road ahead. The Lady Galadriel gives Frodo and Sam the opportunity to look into the Mirror of Galadriel, which "shows things that were, things that are, and things that yet may be."[10] In this way they encounter the world of imagination and possibility. Much of it is terrible, but Galadriel and Celeborn bring words and gifts of comfort and hope. They share some wisdom for what the next part of the journey may look like for the companions

5. Tolkien, *Lord of the Rings*, 369.
6. Tolkien, *Lord of the Rings*, 371.
7. Tolkien, *Lord of the Rings*, 390.
8. Tolkien, *Lord of the Rings*, 409.
9. Tolkien, *Lord of the Rings*, 378.
10. Tolkien, *Lord of the Rings*, 381.

and provision them accordingly. Galadriel tells them, "Maybe the paths that you each shall tread are already laid before your feet, though you do not see them."[11]

Theme 1: Sabbath Is About Place, Not Just Time

Typically, when people mention Sabbath, they refer to its boundaries of time. Sabbath is one day of rest following six days of work. However, within the Lothlórien description, there is much more of a focus on description of the place where they are resting rather than on time. Indeed, the passage of time seems incidental, and far more time passes than they thought.

This dualism of time and space (place) is highlighted by Peruvian theologian and physician Hanz Gutierrez in a series of blogs:

> Time without Space has led the modern world to build a new kind of dualism. A temporal dualism of a time that represents the only dimension where meaning can really emerge, against a devaluated space which only needs to be overcome because it is unable to offer a possible place for meaning. And the Sabbath, amputated of its inborn spatial component, seems to be swallowed by this perspective and to have lost its power of renewal.[12]

Thus, a focus on Sabbath as time, without a recognition of place or space, means that it is robbed of its ability to renew our souls. This sense is captured by public theologian Samuel Wells, who describes Sabbath as "being with God," an activity outside of normal human time. He describes it as

> God and humanity in peaceable interaction[,] . . . fundamentally just being, because there is no better place to be and no better company to keep and no better thing to be doing. This is Sabbath—the crown of creation: simply being with God.[13]

---

11. Tolkien, *Lord of the Rings*, 388.
12. Gutierrez, "Spatial Theology (Part 1)," para. 7.
13. Wells, *Nazareth Manifesto*, 26.

There has been a renewed interest in developing theologies of place in the last twenty years and a growth of the idea of urban spirituality. Urban missiologist Karina Kreminski captures the importance of place and the subversive spiritual practice of slowing down:

> We can find the sacred spaces in our city and practise rest. In the city, there are places that people go to in order to stop, reflect, eat and slow down. They are usually parks or places that are beautified by nature. Sometimes these sacred spaces can be buildings or monuments that hold special significance for the community.[14]

She contrasts this with the sacred places of Christendom: cathedrals and churches, which are rejected by a society that rejects the evil such institutions have come to represent the abuse of children, greed, power, and exclusivity. In this way, "we more clearly see that the sacred spills out onto the streets, mixing with the horror and beauty of humanity. The horror mixes with the profane, heaven touches dirt, and peace mingles with turbulence."[15]

We see the importance of place in nonurban environments also. Poet and farmer Wendell Berry uses his Sabbath poems to celebrate a particular place—his farm in Kentucky. This land is described as a paradise, where heaven touches earth, a sacred place, a place of spiritual encounter,[16] as in the 1991 Sabbath poem: "Amid the woods: a farm / Little enough to see / Or call across—cornfield / Hayfield and pasture, clear / As if remembered, dreamed / And yearned for long ago . . . As on a sabbath walk."[17]

In Scripture, we recognise the importance of "place" to God. We note the love with which God created this place on which we live, the world: "God saw all that he had made, and it was very good" (Gen 1:31).[18] Place was significant in the covenant made to

---

14. Kreminski, *Urban Spirituality*, 201.

15. Kreminski, *Urban Spirituality*, 128.

16. Hudson, "Instantaneous and Eternal," 183.

17. Berry, "1991, IX," in *This Day*, 114–15, quoted in Hudson, "Instantaneous and Eternal," 183.

18. All Scripture quotations in this chapter are taken from the NIV.

Abraham—and has always been significant to God's people—as he was told to go "to the land I will show you" (Gen 12:1). As he told Moses, it was a "good and spacious land, a land flowing with milk and honey" (Exod 3:8). Jerusalem was identified as the city where God's presence would be experienced in the temple: "For the glory of the Lord filled his temple" (1 Kgs 8:11).

Jesus was born into a specific place, Bethlehem, as foretold by the prophets: "But you, Bethlehem Ephrathah, though you are small among the clans of Judah, out of you will come for me one who will be ruler over Israel, whose origins are from of old, from ancient times" (Mic 5:2). And God, through John, reveals details of the new creation, a tangible place where he will dwell with his people: "Look! God's dwelling-place is now among the people, and he will dwell with them. They will be his people, and God himself will be with them and be their God" (Rev 21:3). As writer and editor RuthAnne Irvin points out, "God spoke the world into being, into places."[19] And God continues to be known in place, as well as time.

Indeed, pastor and theologian A. J. Swoboda asserts that frequently Sabbath-keeping is related to land well-being (Lev 26:3–5).[20] In Lev 26:33–34 it says, "The land will rest and enjoy its sabbath years." This is reinforced by 2 Chr 36:21 in a commentary on what happened while the Israelites were in exile: "The land enjoyed its sabbath rests; all the time of its desolation it rested, until the seventy years were completed in fulfilment of the word of the Lord spoken by Jeremiah."

God's interest in place is one of the arguments made by Christians for creation care. The reality is that our choices impact the places around us, and as Christian environmentalist Laura M. Hartman contends, we need the Sabbath to remind us to care for the places God has given us; hence Sabbath-keeping is an environmental as well as a spiritual practice. Building on Jurgen Moltmann's suggestion that the Sabbath should be a day of new creation

19. Irvin, "Redeeming Home," 77.
20. Swoboda, *Subversive Sabbath*, 131–32.

and ecological rest when we cease from polluting the world, when she writes,

> Sabbath-keeping not only has the potential to inculcate environmental habits and attitudes, but it also can constitute a fulfilling expression of those habits and attitudes, a way of nurturing environmental practice and perspectives.[21]

This human impact on place is picked up by Berry in his Sabbath poems, which increasingly notice human mistreatment of place: "You will see that your place, wherever it is . . . bears the shadow of its destruction by war / which is the economy of greed which is plunder."[22]

This awareness is echoed by Swoboda, who asserts that we are meant to live in intimate relationship with the land, and Sabbath is an opportunity to reestablish that relationship, to care for creation.[23]

However, sometimes what is needed is not activism, but . . . simply . . . ceasing—*shabbat*—a lesson that was learnt during the COVID lockdowns when the land recovered and animals returned.[24] More significantly, ceasing begins to deal with the greed in human hearts that drives consumption and overproduction that harms the land. As Swoboda suggests, "Our culture says that healing can only come by doing. Scripture tells a different story. The world is healed by our stopping."[25] This is what is so subversive about the Sabbath; it attacks our idolatry of self—that we must save the world—which is the root of all sin. Swoboda explains this fuller gospel message, "As a missionary I have sensed that part of

---

21. Hartman, "Christian Sabbath-Keeping," 62–63.

22. Berry, "2003, III," in *This Day*, 239–40, quoted in Hudson, "Instantaneous and Eternal," 183.

23. Swoboda, *Subversive Sabbath*, 134.

24. Some of these environmental impacts are documented in Bar, "COVID-19 Lockdown."

25. Swoboda, *Subversive Sabbath*, 135.

my role is not only helping connect people to the life of Jesus but also connecting them to the land that Jesus created."[26]

As well as recognizing that Sabbath is about place, not just about time, we need to recognise that Sabbath is also about creating a space—not just for rest—but for contemplation.

Theme 2: Sabbath Is About Contemplation, Not Just Rest

In Lothlórien, it was only when the company experienced deep physical rest and healing from their hurts that they were able to have space for emotional expression, experiencing their deep grief at the loss of their guide Gandalf, who had disappeared dramatically in the Mines of Moria. Their hosts in Lothlorien joined them in lament, in speech and song. "Often they heard nearby Elvish voices singing, and knew that they were making songs of lamentation for his fall, for they caught his name among the sweet sad words that they could not understand."[27]

Much Sabbath literature focuses on the need for physical rest, apparently ignoring the fact that God modeled the Sabbath for us (Gen 2:2), even though he never gets tired—indeed, "he who watches over you will not slumber" (Ps 121:3). This raises the possibility of Sabbath as being about creating space in our normal routine not just for rest but space for contemplation. Contemplation is deep reflection in the presence of God that naturally leads to worship.

This theme is captured by pastor Adam Mabry, who describes Sabbath rest as an art, "an expressive form of the personal experience of rest in King Jesus. It has power both to reveal and reshape. It lays bare our biggest hopes and solidifies our truest longings."[28]

Perhaps this makes more sense of philosopher Dallas Willard's famous comment to mentee John Ortberg that "hurry is the biggest enemy of spiritual formation," which is captured in turn

---

26. Swoboda, *Subversive Sabbath*, 136.

27. Tolkien, *Lord of the Rings*, 378.

28. Mabry, *Art of Rest*, 131.

by Ortberg's mentee John Mark Comer in the title of his book *The Ruthless Elimination of Hurry*.[29] As we rush through the modern life, we need to create spaces where we can pay attention—to God, to the world around us, and to what is happening within us.

This is beautifully captured in a story told by Irish poet John O'Donahue in his book *Anam Cara*; he describes a European explorer who was travelling with African helpers. After three days the Africans refused to go on, explaining, "We have moved too quickly to reach here; now we need to wait to give our spirits a chance to catch up with us."[30] Perhaps all of us have not noticed how quickly we move through this world.

Returning to Wells's idea of Sabbath as "being with God," we can see the connection with the need to create space for such contemplation of God. This is the resistance idea captured by Old Testament scholar Walter Brueggemann in his seminal work on Sabbath—resisting the movements of the world that crowd God out, that focus on ourselves, that distract us from our one true love and purpose. Brueggemann says,

> Divine rest on the seventh day of creation has made clear (a) that YHWH is not a workaholic, (b) that YHWH is not anxious about the full functioning of creation, and (c) that the well-being of creation does not depend on endless work.[31]

Being freed from the endless demands of work, we stop and contemplate God, ourselves, one another, and the world in which he has placed us. This is not easy for us; as therapist Dan Allender challenges, "Do we really believe that sabbath delight is God's heart for us? Are we willing to silence the rabble of idols and foul spirits to hear the intoxicating joy of God?"[32] He affirms that Sabbath is meant to be a time of delighting, in God and in his people and in his creation.

29. Ortberg, *Soul Keeping*, 20; see Comer, *Ruthless Elimination of Hurry*, 19.

30. O'Donohue, *Anam Cara*, 151.

31. Brueggemann, *Sabbath as Resistance*, 6.

32. Allender, *Sabbath*, 193.

Gutierrez is in sympathy with this idea in his "Spatial Theology," which

> Doesn't aspire to approach things, persons and events by using Space as a kind of ordering and neutralizing instrument. On the contrary, Space becomes the place of freedom and interaction. Place makes the world grounded by bringing beings together without the dictatorship of time.[33]

It is a movement from pragmatic concerns to one of freedom and encounter.

Poet and author David Whyte points to the need for such contemplation and the impact on us: "Rested, we are ready for the world but not held hostage by it; rested, we care again for the right things and the right people in the right way. In rest we re-establish the goals that makes us more generous, more courageous, more of an invitation."[34]

Having encountered God in place, and experienced him in deep contemplation, we are ready to begin to reimagine our place in the world, with God and with others.

Theme 3: Sabbath Is About Imagination, Not Just Worship

In Lothlórien, the company have found a beautiful place and have experienced deep rest, not just of their bodies but of their minds and hearts. They are now freed to imagine, to find a way forward in their journey. Until now, they have been reacting—to news of doom, problems around them, attacks from enemies. However, in this time of Sabbath, they are freed to move beyond hurry and fear and to see the world in new ways.

In addition to a focus on time, and rest, the third aspect of Sabbath that is generally emphasized is that of worship. In worship, we recall all that God has done and name his characteristics that lead us to love him more. However, Sabbath allows us to go

33. Gutierrez, "Spatial Theology (Part 4)," para. 10.
34. Whyte, *Consolations*, 134–35.

beyond worship for the sake of the past and present, and to begin to encounter the future. How will our story align with God's purposes as we move forward?

Hartman picks up on this idea, pointing out that "in keeping the Sabbath, Christians are living 'as if': living the 'already' of God's reign even in a still fallen, 'not yet' world. In observing the Sabbath, Christians' desires and habits may be continually formed by this spiritual practice to be more in keeping with God's will for the world."[35] Thus Sabbath allows us to live into the future, into the new creation of our imagination.

South African theologians Pieter G. R. de Villiers and George Marchinkowski link the three themes, which they explain as a "spiritual tale" about God

> who gives time and space to humanity in which they experience the joy of the divine presence, providence and care as it is to be detected in the world. . . . Work is suspended and rest is needed in order to be reminded of and to celebrate the aesthetic nature and significance of life and creation.[36]

The aesthetic and the significant are both characteristics of imagination. We are moved by creativity and beauty to imagine a purpose beyond ourselves—a different way of being—made possible by being removed from the ordinariness of everyday life but also grounded in the reality of that ordinary life.

Berry captures this tension perfectly; his Sabbath imagination is not always future focused but intensely now: "Heaven is only present / instantaneous and eternal / a mayfly, a blue day-flower / a life entirely given / complete forever in its hour."[37]

As fellow poet/writer Whyte describes it, "We are rested when we are a living exchange between what lies inside and what lies outside, when we are an intriguing conversation between the

---

35. Hartman, "Christian Sabbath-Keeping," 62–63.

36. De Villiers and Marchinkowski, "Sabbath-Keeping in the Bible," 4.

37. Berry, "2008, VIII," in *This Day*, 322, quoted in Hudson, "Instantaneous and Eternal," 191.

potential that lies in our imagination and the possibilities for making that internal image real in the world."[38]

Entrepreneurial professor Denise Daniels and author Shannon Vandewarker talk about the necessity of being freed from distraction to enable such imagining by focusing on Deut 5:12–15, where God requires the Israelites to remember that they were freed by him from being slaves so they no longer *have* to work seven days, and they can "reflect on the goodness of God in their midst, and . . . put away their productive pursuits."[39] This reflection process, they suggest, could be future oriented but only if we are not "busy, tired, overwhelmed, or distracted."[40] In this way, Sabbath rest begets the ability to do Sabbath imagination.

Pastor and professor Mark Buchanan also sees Sabbath as a call to imagination, "an attempt to awaken in you new ways of perceiving this world, fresh ways of understanding your place and God's presence in it."[41] This is such an important and under-emphasized element of Sabbath, desperately needed by harried corporate executives, frustrated frontline workers, and bored carers alike. We need the space to step out of the ordinary routines of our lives to reimagine what could be, what should be . . . a kingdom perspective.

However, Brueggemann will not leave us satisfied with such a purely individualistic focus toward Sabbath, which he describes as "not simply a pause. It is an occasion for reimagining all social life away from coercion and compassion to compassionate solidarity. . . . Sabbath is not simply the pause that refreshes. It is the pause that transforms."[42]

Thus, Sabbath is never just a personal spiritual experience but an opportunity to focus on those around us, to build on relationships (as Sara Minard will build on in her chapter). Later,

---

38. Whyte, *Consolations*, 133.

39. Daniels and Vandewarker, *Working in the Presence of God*, 191.

40. Daniels and Vandewarker, *Working in the Presence of God*, 195.

41. Buchanan, *Rest of God*, 4.

42. Brueggemann, *Sabbath as Resistance*, 45.

Brueggemann particularly calls us to a Sabbath reflection on "the most vulnerable of neighbours."[43]

In reflecting on the Heb 4 description of the people entering God's Sabbath rest, Buchanan resonates with the idea of imagining heaven touching earth. "Sabbath isn't eternity, but it's close. It's a kind of precinct of heaven. . . . In finding the rest of God now, we prepare for the fullness of God one day."[44] As Wells summarizes it, Sabbath "is an intimation of the world to come."[45]

The arc of the biblical consideration of Sabbath is from a particular place and time in Gen 1 to an invitation from God to live into the future rest we will experience in new creation. "There remains, then, a Sabbath-rest for the people of God; for anyone who enters God's rest also rests from their works, just as God did from his" (Heb 4:9–10). We benefit from the renewal of that rest, but we also use it as an opportunity to imagine the new creation possibilities for our work.

As well as imagination for the future, Swoboda focuses on the present, citing Ps 19 to point out that the Sabbath helps us to stop and appreciate the beauty around us, God's work in creating the land. Indeed, creation can also teach us about God, "revealing knowledge" (Ps 19:2). Thus, the Sabbath appreciation of creation gives us an insight into the imagination of God.[46]

How do we stop in the crazy busyness of our world with its relentless striving? John Mark Comer is perhaps the most pragmatic of the writers this chapter has considered. As pastor of an urban church, he is anxious to help his congregation members who are endlessly busy and hurrying. He lists sixteen items of restfulness versus relentlessness; and several relate to the conditions necessary for imagination. Sabbath enables us to enter the restfulness of delight (rather than distraction), clarity (rather than confusion), trust (rather than worry), and joy (rather than sadness).[47]

43. Brueggemann, *Sabbath as Resistance*, 71.
44. Buchanan, *Rest of God*, 213.
45. Wells, *Nazareth Manifesto*, 69.
46. Swoboda, *Subversive Sabbath*, 141.
47. Comer, *Ruthless Elimination of Hurry*, 149.

Fellow urban pastor Rich Villodas picks up on this idea of trust as a prerequisite for such imagining. He points out that Sabbath is a time when we leave work incomplete as an act of trust that points forward: "In the practice of sabbath keeping, we live out the truth that one day we will leave all things unfinished as we rest in the arms of Jesus."[48] In this way, Sabbath is a form of surrender to God, trusting him to care for what is unfinished, allowing us to imagine all that could be possible dwelling in his presence.

Leaving Lothlórien, Ending Sabbath

When Frodo and the company left Lothlórien they still had a long way to go, with many hazards and losses ahead. "Lórien was slipping backward, like a bright ship masted with enchanted trees, sailing on forgotten shores, while they sat helpless upon the margin of the grey and leafless world."[49]

For hobbits and elves, dwarves and humans, recapturing the lost wonders of Sabbath—sacred place, sacred space for contemplation, and sacred imagination—may enable a greater experience of renewal, helping us to understand more fully what Jesus meant when he said, "The Sabbath was made for mortal, not mortal for the Sabbath" (Mark 2:27).

However, there will be a sense that the joys and delights of the Sabbath make us more conscious of the deficiencies of this sin-saturated world, a "grey and leafless world" in comparison. May that make us even more inspired—when our Sabbath has ended—to work with God to bring the kingdom alive on earth "as it is in heaven" (Matt 6:10) in our ordinary work and ordinary workplaces.

This suggests that Sabbath and its many gifts are not just for the people of God; they are intrinsic to what it means to be human and essential to what it means to live fully in this world, and the new creation.

48. Villodas, *Deeply Formed Life*, 34.
49. Tolkien, *Lord of the Rings*, 397.

Bibliography

Allender, Dan B. *Sabbath: The Ancient Practices.* Nashville: Thomas Nelson, 2010.

Bar, Harekrishna. "COVID-19 Lockdown: Animal Life, Ecosystem and Atmospheric Environment." *Environment, Development and Sustainability* 23.6 (2021) 8161–78. https://doi.org/10.1007/s10668-020-01002-7.

Berry, Wendell. *This Day: Collected and New Sabbath Poems.* Berkeley, CA: Counterpoint, 2013.

Brueggemann, Walter. *Sabbath as Resistance: New Edition with Study Guide.* Louisville: Westminster John Knox Press, 2017.

Buchanan, Mark. *The Rest of God: Restoring Your Soul by Restoring Sabbath.* Nashville: Thomas Nelson, 2007.

Comer, John Mark. *The Ruthless Elimination of Hurry: How to Stay Emotionally Healthy and Spiritually Alive in the Chaos of the Modern World.* London: Hodder & Stoughton, 2019.

Daniels, Denise, and Shannon Vandewarker. *Working in the Presence of God: Spiritual Practices for Everyday Work.* Peabody, MA: Hendrickson, 2019.

De Villiers, Pieter G. R., and George Marchinkowski. "Sabbath-Keeping in the Bible from the Perspective of Biblical Spirituality." *HTS Teologiese Studies / Theological Studies* 77.2 (2021) 1–8. https://doi.org/10.4102/hts. v77i2.6755.

Gutierrez, Hanz. "A Spatial Theology of the Sabbath: Time over Space? (Part 1)." *Spectrum Magazine,* Aug. 8, 2019. https://spectrummagazine.org/ views/2019/spatial-theology-sabbath-time-over-space-part-1.

———. "A Spatial Theology of the Sabbath: Time over Space? (Part 4)." *Spectrum Magazine,* Feb. 13, 2020. https://spectrummagazine.org/views/ spatial-theology-sabbath-part-4-world-living-things/.

Hartman, Laura. "Christian Sabbath-Keeping as a Spiritual and Environmental Practice." *Worldviews* 15.1 (2011) 47–64. https://doi. org/10.1163/156853511X553769.

Hudson, Marc. "Instantaneous and Eternal." *Sewanee Review* 123.1 (Winter 2015) 182–91.

Irvin, RuthAnne. "Redeeming Home: A Christian Theology of Place in a Placeless World." Southern Equip. Aug. 8, 2017. https://equip.sbts.edu/ publications/journals/augustine-collegiate-review/acr-11-%20summer/ redeeming-home-christian-theology-place-placeless-world/.

Kreminski, Karina. *Urban Spirituality: Embodying God's Mission in the Neighborhood.* Skyforest, CA: Urban Loft, 2018.

Mabry, Adam. *The Art of Rest: Faith to Hit Pause in a World That Never Stops.* Epsom, Surrey: Good Book, 2018.

O'Donohue, John. *Anam Cara: Spiritual Wisdom from the Celtic World.* London: Bantam, 1998.

Ortberg, John. *Soul Keeping: Caring for the Most Important Part of You.* Grand Rapids: Zondervan, 2014.

Pieters, Timo. "The Christian Symbolism in The Lord of the Rings." European Academy on Religion and Society. Oct. 20, 2021. https://europeanacademyofreligionandsociety.com/news/the-christian-symbolism-in-the-lord-of-the-rings/.

Rubin, Merle. "When the Mind Falls into Rhythm." *Los Angeles Times*, Feb. 9, 2004. https://www.latimes.com/archives/la-xpm-2004-feb-09-et-book9-story.html.

Swoboda, A. J. *Subversive Sabbath: The Surprising Power of Rest in a Nonstop World*. Grand Rapids: Brazos, 2018.

Tolkien, J. R. R. *The Lord of the Rings*. London: Unwin, 1978.

Villodas, Rich. *The Deeply Formed Life: Five Transformative Values to Root Us in the Way of Jesus*. Colorado Springs: WaterBrook, 2020.

Wells, Samuel. *A Nazareth Manifesto: Being with God*. Oxford: Wiley Blackwell, 2015.

Whyte, David. *Consolations: The Solace, Nourishment and Underlying Meaning of Everyday Words*. Edinburgh: Canongate, 2019.

Chapter Eight

Sabbath as Renewal

C. Sara Lawrence Minard

There is no wealth but life. —John Ruskin

It is only with the heart that one can see rightly; what is essential is invisible to the eyes. —Antoine de Saint-Exupery

Introduction

THE US SURGEON GENERAL, Dr. Vivek Murthy, recently published a report revealing the devastating news that never in human history have Americans been more lonely, isolated, or depressed.[1] Half of all adults experience measurable levels of loneliness, according to pre-COVID survey data, and an estimated 8 percent of adults and 18 percent of teenagers experience major depressive disorder (MDD). Dr. Murthy calls this a national health crisis because "the disconnection [with people] fundamentally affects our mental, physical, and societal health." In fact, the report notes, "loneliness

1. US Surgeon General, "Advisory."

115

and isolation increase the risk for individuals to develop mental health challenges in their lives, and lacking connection can increase the risk for premature death to levels comparable to smoking daily."[2]

It sends a strong signal that something is very wrong when it takes the surgeon general to notify a nation that it needs to prioritize relationships "as a source of healing and well-being hidden in plain sight, if we are to live healthier, more fulfilled, and more productive lives."[3] What are the root causes of this public health crisis whereby we have stopped investing our time and energy in developing meaningful human relationships? What are we afraid of, or too busy doing? Is it that most of us are overworked and underpaid, unable to save and invest for the future and looking for an escape?[4] Maybe it is the emptiness that comes from our addiction to the unfulfilling pings and dings from our phones and social media accounts, tricking us into a false sense of belonging, purpose, and meaning? Or maybe it is our overreliance on convenience in this modern, online world, where everything is only a mouse click away, while we ignore the living, breathing earth that is choking on the carbon we are emitting?

While there is clearly no one single explanation for any public health crisis, especially as complex as this one, there is little doubt (ask anyone with a cell phone) the dependence on the technology in our pocket is partly to blame for our increasing inability to "find the time" to invest in more meaningful offline relationships, let alone connect with nature and our community, all of which are in a state of disrepair. Thus, it is worthwhile investigating the ubiquitous nature of technology, as Andy Crouch does in *The Life We're Looking For: Reclaiming Relationship in a Technological World*, and explore what he terms "the loneliness of a personalized world."[5]

With the prevalence of social media, our most basic human need for belonging gets hijacked by limiting beliefs and superficial

2. US Surgeon General, "Advisory," para. 1.
3. US Surgeon General, "Advisory," para. 2.
4. International Labor Organization, "Americans Work Longest Hours."
5. Crouch, *Life We're Looking For*, 3.

measures of performance, leading to "othering" people to elevate one's own identity in the quest to be seen in a quasi-anonymous virtual reality. We are seeing this personalized-but-never-personal online environment lead to behaviors that are damaging our young people. Motivated by this fear of not being seen, this need to have constant attention leads to violence towards self or others. Fear of not being enough is easily amplified by any type of economic uncertainty, especially when the promise of happiness or prosperity from professional success, online status, or individual freedom does not deliver us. We see this especially among working class middle-aged white men in the US who are more susceptible to being recruited by extremists and more likely to commit suicide than any other population group in the country.[6] We are *relationally bankrupt*.

At the same time, we are all experiencing the effects of extreme income inequality,[7] the likes of which have never been seen before. All Americans, albeit to extremely varying degrees, experience the illusion of scarcity that drives consumerism in a market economy, both in ways known and unknown to us. What we are sure of, however, is that these forces are shaping our choices, influencing our behavior, and incentivizing us to prioritize what we love in ways that don't always align with what is most important to us.

As economic historian Avner Offer explains, our need for belonging drives our economic behavior and is measured by "regard," or by how we are seen by others:

> Personal interaction ranks very high among the sources of satisfaction. It can take many forms: acknowledgement, attention, acceptance, respect, reputation, status, power, intimacy, love, friendship, kinship, sociability. To wrap it all into one term, [economic] interaction is driven by the grant and pursuit of regard. In *The Theory*

6. Graham, *Power of Hope*, 14.
7. Saez and Zucman, "Rise of Income and Wealth Inequality," 3–26.

of Moral Sentiments, Adam Smith described the purpose of economic activity as the acquisition of regard.[8]

Meanwhile, the "haves" are still trying to convince the "have nots" to believe in the myth of American meritocracy, that the "dream" can be achieved if you *just work harder*. As Michael Sandel powerfully writes in *The Tyranny of Merit: What's Become of the Common Good?*,

> Even a fair meritocracy, one without cheating or bribery or special privileges for the wealthy, induces the mistaken impression that we have made it on our own. Besides being self-deluding, such thinking is also corrosive of civic sensibilities. For the more we think of ourselves as self-made and self-sufficient, the harder it is to learn gratitude and humility. And without these sentiments, it is hard to care for the common good.[9]

Economic inequality breeds disillusionment and frustration of the sort Sandel explains, and it can quickly turn into resentment, anger, and despair. When coupled with increased uncertainty about impending climate catastrophes and other social stresses, it leaves us feeling lonely and hopeless.

While all the different social, economic, physical, and ecological crises deserve equal attention, on a biblical level, and on a socioeconomic level, one of the biggest crises is a spiritual one: the belief in the false narrative that people can build resilience to life's challenges without authentic relationships. For this reason, there is no more urgent time as this to focus our attention on Sabbath, the Judeo-Christian practice of "ceasing" and reengaging in contemplation and reflection. By investing in a relationship with God's divine presence, we restore an intimate connection with the self, between the self and living things, and between the self and the living God.

---

8. Offer, "Between Gift and Market," 451; cf. 450–76.
9. Sandel, *Tyranny of Merit*, 14.

A Socioeconomic Perspective on Sabbath as Renewal

This chapter presents a *socioeconomic perspective* on the biblical tradition of Sabbath, as the reminder of the intrinsic value of relationships, and the recognition that a Sabbath economics is within our reach. It is useful to note that the term "socio" in socioeconomic, while not excluding sociology, by definition engages with the wider moral and intellectual as well as the purely economic origins of poverty and inequality; it includes major segments of sociology, psychology, geography, anthropology, history, and political science—the whole complex of disciplines that have examined the relationships between society and the economy. It assumes the role of collective organization and social institutions, as pivotal for every form of economic and social organization, is built on some symbolic foundation from which it derives value, meaning, and inspiration.

To do this, we will look, on the one hand, at the interplay between economics—specifically, the loss of moral philosophy in economic thinking—and what the Bible tells us about observing Sabbath economics, and on the other hand, the rise of loneliness, isolation, and related mental health issues currently overtaking American society in the forms of anxiety, loneliness, and depression.

While it would be impossible to establish any direct cause-effect relationship between economic thinking that influences personal and marketplace behavior and the current disturbing trends in physical and psychological well-being in the US, there are four possible socioeconomic dimensions of this interplay that can be observed, and where, I will argue, a Sabbath practice of revaluing relationships and renewing our economic mindsets can be immediately useful.

The first dimension to look at is the limitations of market rationality and the commodification of nature; second, the crisis of hopelessness in the face of rising income and wealth inequality; third, a corporate work culture that leads to dehumanization and burnout; and fourth, the loss of social capital as trust in communities and social institutions is eroded.

After examining these four dimensions, we will look at how the economics of Sabbath can serve as a bridge between our current public health crisis and our universally shared desire for relationships, authentic connection, belonging, and hope. What ideas, for example, of an embodied practice of Sabbath can offer new ways of engaging in a more just and sustainable economy and offer hope for a population suffering from an epidemic of loneliness? How can ancient practices of observing Sabbath practically cultivate the heart, body, and mind in today's noisy world and give us a deeper appreciation of what matters? What needs to be prioritized in our socioeconomic decision making to restore the intrinsic value of authentic, life-giving human connections, so vital to renewing our mental, physical, and societal health? How might we use technology, time, and money to achieve such equanimity? How might a new understanding of Sabbath, as embodied in Jesus' teachings and hidden in plain sight, provide a source of healing and well-being, and in turn, help re-prioritize what we love, help us find peace in contemplative stillness, help to reframe the purpose of money, and help bring a sense of abundance to our lives?

In conclusion, I will suggest that *Sabbath can be a prism* through which we can choose to develop a more comprehensive, kingdom-centered view of economics, intentionally working to prioritize the intrinsic value and worth of the things most important to us, and continually learning how to renew our relationships with God, self, and neighbor. By "seeking first" these deeper relationships, we can create a more beloved community and a more resilient planet, filling body, mind, soul, and spirit with the gift of God's love, beauty, and grace. But living is hard, and the world is on fire, and one in five teenagers feel hopeless, and so, as public theologian Howard Thurman proclaimed, "This is perhaps the greatest challenge that the religion of Jesus faces in modern times."[10]

---

10. Thurman, *Jesus and the Disinherited*, 58.

The Limitations of Market Rationality and the Commodification of Nature

Born in 1819, renowned art critic, moral philosopher, and writer John Ruskin became a leading opponent in his day of classical political economy and Victorian capitalism. He was witnessing the British economic system rationalize the despoiling of nature and the debasement of living human beings and how this was increasingly being reflected in the representation of mankind and nature in art.[11] His most famous writing, *Unto This Last*, was read by Mahatma Gandhi during his time in South Africa, and it apparently changed Gandhi's life instantly and became the basis of his work on nonviolence.

What is important about Ruskin is that he starts his critique of economics with his own definitions, disregarding conventional lexicon and offering a new definition of wealth. It is the premise from which all else flows: Wealth is life. This view of wealth would be shared by theologian, renowned organist, doctor, and humanitarian (and winner of the 1953 Nobel Peace Prize) Albert Schweitzer, when he coined the phrase "reverence for life."[12] Asking the same moral philosophy question as Ruskin, Schweitzer devoted his life to a calling he heard from his hospital in a remote village in Gabon: how is what I am doing consistent with my ethical affirmation of the world and of life?[13]

Raised by an evangelical Christian mother and an art and literary father, Ruskin recited both testaments of the Bible every year, eventually committed Adam Smith's *Theory of Moral Sentiments* to memory, and reread Plato and Dante as he matured. His evangelicalism was expressed in several notions that remain central to practical theology and modern economics in the twenty-first century: stewardship, human flourishing, and a rejection of *homo economicus*. He became disillusioned, as many Christians are today, by what he saw as religion's inability to address the harsh realities of

11. Spear and Parramore, "What Is Real Wealth?"
12. See Schweitzer, selection from *Out of My Life and Thought*, 12.
13. Schweitzer, selection from *Out of my Life and Thought*.

inequities and injustices in the division of labor. Ruskin's insights into what constitutes a just and equitable relationship between people, work, and wealth in the economic sphere were most likely informed by Eph 2:7–10: "Through His goodness revealed to us in Christ Jesus, he shows us how infinitely rich God is in grace, saving us by pure gift . . . so that we are God's work of art, created in Christ Jesus to live the good life as from the beginning he had meant us to live it."[14] We are, as Ruskin and the apostle Paul remind us, equal recipients of grace destined to live the good life in Jesus.

What is especially pertinent about Ruskin's socioeconomic ideas that make them a helpful bridge to Sabbath economics is that they start with first principles, which means they don't take assumptions of self-interest or rational choice for granted. Instead, they transcend the capitalism/Marxism dichotomy while rejecting the atomization of working people. His moral positions align with Scottish philosopher Adam Smith in that, for him, wealth is not morally neutral—it is *relational*; it is not utilitarian. He rejects any notion that wealth is transactional or that work should be associated with payment of debts, particularly for those without wealth.

Centuries and continents apart from Ruskin, one Kentucky farmer, writer, and poet, Wendell Berry, wrote an essay titled "Two Economies," wherein he notes "the thing that troubles us about the industrial economy is exactly that it is not comprehensive enough, that, moreover, it tends to destroy what it does not comprehend, and that it is *dependent* upon much that it does not comprehend."[15] He goes on to compare the modern industrial economy, to what he later in the essay calls the Great Economy, the kingdom of God:

> Without presuming too much [the] first principle of the Kingdom of God is that it includes everything; in it, the fall of every sparrow is a significant event. We are in it whether we know it or not and whether we wish it or not. Another principle, both ecological and traditional, is that everything in the Kingdom of God is joined both to it and to everything else that is in it; that is to say, the

14. Scripture quotations throughout this chapter are taken from the NIV.
15. Berry, *Home Economics*, 55 (emphasis original).

Kingdom of God is orderly. A third principle is that humans do not and can never know either all the creatures that the Kingdom of God contains or the whole pattern or order by which it contains them. . . . The difficulty of our predicament, then, is made clear if we add a fourth principle: Though we cannot produce a complete or even an adequate description of this order, severe penalties are in store for us if we presume upon it or violate it.[16]

Berry expands his critique beyond the biblical, evoking the Greek name for the pride that attempts to transcend human limitations, *hubris*, to explain how God used the Sabbath to demonstrate to the Israelites the importance of accepting their dependence on God. Berry then draws on the sixth chapter of the book of Matthew, where Jesus tells us not to question where our food or drink or clothes will come from, but instead, "seek ye first the Kingdom of God, and his righteousness, and all these things will be added unto you" (Matt 6:31–33). This is a big leap of faith for most people in any economy, but as Berry argues, in our modern capitalist economy, "people can add value to things, we may transform trees into boards, but there will always be a primary value to things that we cannot see," let alone price. "We did not make trees, or the intelligence and talent of workers," and yet we give value to them based on their perceived utility, often blind to their intrinsic value in use, and worth. In some cases, we altogether ignore the interdependences of living things in relation to each other, such are the vast unknowns that constitute the mystery of God's perfect and comprehensive Great Economy.[17]

In the mid – to late-eighteenth century, Adam Smith wrote in his most important work, *The Theory of Moral Sentiments*,

> No matter how selfish you think man is, it's obvious that there are some principles in his nature that give him an interest in the welfare of others, and make their

16. Berry, *Home Economics*, 65–66.
17. Berry, *Home Economics*, 56–57.

happiness necessary to him, even if he gets nothing from it but the pleasure of seeing it.[18]

Referring to the Greek root word for economics, *oikos*, which means household, Adam Smith did not consider an exchange of labor for money as necessarily adhering to any different set of moral arrangements than, say, the exchange of services for public benefit. He understood that, in all cases, what was of value to one person may be different for another, and yet, one can still appreciate this difference and agree that all people in a society (the household), regardless of their activity, merit sufficient care and services. Considered by many as the father of economics, Smith fundamentally believed in a moral purpose to all economic activity, which is not self-aggrandizement or the accumulation of capital but the ability to care for and have genuine concern for the common good and love of neighbor.[19]

Two hundred years later, in response to the Great Depression, Franklin Delano Roosevelt's New Deal, a bold policy response to a devastating financial crisis, emphasized the essential role of welfare in stabilizing an economy and used the powerful levers of government to correct market failures, echoing the need for prioritization of the intrinsic value of relationships as evidenced by Smith, Ruskin, Schweitzer, Berry, and the apostle Paul. Keynesian economics, which stabilized the economy, promoted full employment, and managed aggregate demand using supply-side economics, was challenged partly as a political response to the rise of communism. Hayek and others, who disagreed with public welfare, promoted the benefits of free market capitalism, and free market theories like

18. Smith, *Theory of Moral Sentiments*.

19. It is not often corrected, so we will set the record straight here: the common understanding of Adam Smith as a proponent of unbridled self-interest and free markets is not accurate. He was equally concerned with other regarding behavior, where self-interest could not be seen as separate from natural love and affection (approbation) for others as the driving factors of human behavior; he wrote of other regarding behavior over forty times in his book *Theory of Moral Sentiments*. He describes forces of supply and demand as an invisible hand once when discussing the threats of mercantilism in the *Wealth of Nations*.

monetarism, which became the hallmarks of democracy. Unfortunately, the technical expertise and political will required to reign in public spending fabricated faulty premises from which harmful policies were generated. As economics became increasingly divorced from moral philosophy, and, consequently, immune to ethics as taught across religions and the humanities, economic ideas that prioritized free markets, equating capital accumulation with unfettered rugged individualism, turned into policies that further entrenched social inequalities, deepened divisions based on material wealth, and shielded wealth holders from scrutiny and responsibility.

Since at least the 1970s, the economics discipline has abandoned its Smithian roots of positioning social welfare and the natural world as central to market functioning. We may shudder at the idea of social obligations in a free-market economy, but we mistakenly confuse policies that support an economy of care and other forms of welfare economics with socialism and other forms of state-controlled markets. However, as social mobility disappears and we see the highest rates of inequality on record, the social contract that was the American dream has been denied, in large part because, as economic historian Avner Offer writes, "the interests of the rich can be at odds with those of the rest. Without reciprocal entitlement, the role of the many is to service the few, with no confidence of being cared for in return."[20]

Theologians like Ched Myers offer helpful biblical perspectives on Sabbath economics from a pastoral and community-based perspective, framing Sabbath as liberatory in how it addresses market failures such as extreme income and wealth inequality. Myers's work challenges Christians who want to separate their faith from their money by reframing the image of Jesus on the cross not as transactional but as a gift of transformation.[21] Recalling Ruskin's critique of commercial capital accumulation, it "may be indicative, on the one hand, of faithful industries, progressive energies, and productive ingenuities: or, on the other, it may be indicative of

20. Offer, "Economy of Obligation," 5.
21. Myers, *Sabbath Economics*, 1.5; see also Rohr, *Things Hidden*, 51.

moral luxury, merciless tyranny, ruinous chicane."[22] Whether it is the former or the latter, Sabbath economics would say the outcome will be determined by one's view of the cross, how it teaches us what "the good life" means, and how we measure our contribution to human flourishing.

Myers's ministry on Sabbath economics invites Christians to remember that social and economic justice are interwoven into the very fabric of every aspect of the Bible; that we are all economic actors, making moral and ethical decisions with money every day; and that we impact others with the decisions we make. He frames Sabbath economics as follows: "At its root, Sabbath observance is about gift and limits: the grace of receiving that which the creator gives, and the responsibility not to take too much, nor to mistake the gift for a possession."[23]

Although a lapsed evangelical from the nineteenth century, Ruskin, it turns out, was also drawing on Jesus' teaching that there is no wealth but life. When we apply Sabbath as a prism to inform our economic choices, it becomes clear that material wealth could never be a reliable proxy for the intrinsic value and worth of people or the natural world. The economic implication of the Sabbath tradition as articulated in the Bible is that the world created by God is abundant, with enough for everyone—provided that human communities restrain their appetites and live within limits. This implies recognizing how much is "enough" and prioritizing the needs of others. Where *mammon* is understood to negatively describe the pursuit of wealth, *manna* is used to refer to God's abundance and nourishment. The key to understanding Sabbath, then, as the renewal of relationships is in how we support one another in our work and our choices, "de-privatizing our anxieties and communitizing our imaginations."[24]

Humility, therefore, and acceptance of the limitations of what we can and cannot know or understand, coupled with this reverence for the intrinsic value and worth of all living things

---

22. Ruskin, *Unto This Last*, 52.

23. Myers, *Sabbath Economics*, 1.5.

24. Myers, *Sabbath Economics*, 1.5.

as assigned in God's kingdom, are important starting points for understanding Sabbath as a prism and an economic mindset. Sabbath economics requires us to recognize, whether we are farmers, fishers, financiers, teachers, politicians, or scientists, that we are all asset managers, responsible for managing the assets available to each of us, including our mental and physical health, and seeing the natural world as more than an extractive resource. "Nature nurtures and nourishes us, so we must think of natural assets as durable entities that not only have use value but also have intrinsic worth."[25] Once we make this connection, the economics of Sabbath and the economics of biodiversity become the same, and a study in Sabbath economics improves our understanding of the portfolio effects of the true costs of biodiversity loss and, more generally, the true costs associated with choosing mammon over manna as the driving moral philosophy in economic thinking.

As a discipline that shapes global and national policy decisions of the utmost consequence, economics in the twentieth and twenty-first centuries has been advocating for a limited role of government, deregulation of financial markets, and the assumption of an essentially pessimistic view of human nature and an overly optimistic view of businesses and self-regulating markets—which the former treasury secretary under four US presidents, Alan Greenspan, famously admitted under oath has "a flaw . . . in the critical functioning structure that defines how the world works."[26] There have been important global gains in terms of GDP growth since the Industrial Revolution and most countries have seen great prosperity and lightning speed innovations. It has also been a time of unbridled ecological devastation and resource extraction without regard for human and nonhuman communities relying on those resources. Contemporary economic thinking, particularly on sustainable development, assumes humanity to be external to nature and, therefore,

25. Attenborough, foreword to *Economics of Biodiversity*, 1–2.
26. Clark and Treanor, "Greenspan," para. 15.

no study in the economics of technological change has explored the question of what lifestyles are possible . . . given the current dangers facing humanity of global climate change . . . and the unprecedented rate of loss in biological diversity now taking place.[27]

The Crisis of Hopelessness in the Face of Rising Income and Wealth Inequality

Economist Carol Graham, who studies and writes about hope and what she calls "deaths of despair," shares her perspective on a study undertaken by economist Angus Deaton, summarized in a seminal article published in 2015, which found that deaths of despair were most common among lower middle-income whites in their middle age.[28] Essentially, the combined effects of the decline in manufacturing jobs, the decline in marriage rates, both the physical (housing) and psychological displacement, and the opioid crisis has created a perfect storm for hopelessness among the white working class. Graham explains that today, in the US, we're seeing up to almost a million deaths of despair each year if you include the overdose deaths, which have gone up dramatically since 2015.

What is alarming, as Graham's research shows, is that this phenomenon is rather unique to the United States. Some other deindustrializing places—parts of the UK, Russia in the 1980s—have had something like this but nothing on this scale. There is evidence this is impacting, starting from 2015, our life expectancy, which has been on the decline. The US is the only rich country in the world where this is true, and that means that deaths of despair are eroding significant progress that's being made in cancer deaths, in heart disease, and other areas. As mentioned earlier in the chapter, we know that income inequality can generate social strain and exacerbate mental health issues. We know that high levels of inequality can lead to feelings of "othering" and exclusion,

27. Dasgupta, *Economics of Biodiversity*, 11.
28. Graham, *Power of Hope*.

anxiety, depression, affecting both individuals and communities. Economic policies and structures that perpetuate significant disparities in wealth and opportunity can destroy aspirations and hope, weakening community connections and resilience.

The economic implications of practicing the Sabbath include recognizing that the disparities in wealth and power are not "natural" but the result of human sin and must be mitigated within the community of faith through redistribution.[29] Of course, any discussion of wealth redistribution immediately raises hackles, especially for those who have significant wealth and benefit from an economic system that puts a primacy on private ownership. Whereas Ruskin and Smith saw economics as requiring both public services and an economy of care for others as the moral purpose of markets, a more modern evangelical perspective might be the one embodied by Southern minister Jonathan Wilson-Hartgrove, author of *God's Economy: Redefining the Health and Wealth Gospel.*

Wilson-Hartgrove makes the case that how material wealth is accumulated, protected, and invested, with the goal to earn more wealth, is a scarcity mindset and diminishes the gift of abundance from God, who "prepares a banquet table where there is more than enough for anyone who wants to come"[30] and fulfills Jesus' promise in John 10:10, "I came that they may have life and have it abundantly" (NIV). After seeing the abject failure of the church in the marketplace from medieval times, Christians, explains Wilson-Hartgrove, learned to separate their faith (heart) from their economics (money, business, investments), further dividing the spiritual from the material. The inevitable result being the increasing irrelevance of the gospel in everyday life. He continues, "Wealth and poverty both offer their own temptations, but it seems that money has a way of quietly colonizing our imaginations whether we have it or not."[31]

---

29. Myers, *Sabbath Economics Collaborative.*

30. Wilson-Hartgrove, *God's Economy*, 46.

31. Wilson-Hartgrove, *God's Economy*, 41.

A Corporate Work Culture That Leads to Dehumanization and Burnout

The COVID epidemic changed the modern workplace in numerous ways, beginning with the acceptance of remote work, which was a necessity, and an appreciation by most industries of the work-life balance. Unfortunately, we see many of these gains disappearing as the pre-COVID corporate work culture rebounds. It is widely known that certain industries, like finance, law, teaching, and healthcare, are notorious for overworking their workers, which can contribute to physical and mental health challenges. The drive for material success, and the link to financial rewards for worker productivity, can lead to increased work hours, intense internal competition, and high stress on the job. In addition, for women and underrepresented populations, especially marginalized communities, there is the added stress of workplace discrimination. Despite the rise in diversity, equity, and inclusion (DEI) policies, the forces driving competition in a traditional corporate work environment continue to put productivity above human health. This directly impacts people's ability to form and maintain meaningful relationships. We see the negative impact in the largest resignation rate on record, post-COVID, which according to an MIT Sloan Management Review study, can be attributed to toxic and unethical work cultures, which resulted in burnout, anxiety, and other mental health problems across industries.[32] By intentionally embracing Sabbath-based relationship practices that embrace diverse cultures, foster reflective dialogue, and actively address racial and other forms of discrimination and injustice, the workplace can transform from a source of anxiety and stress into an enabling environment for inclusive growth and renewal.

32. Sull et al., "Toxic Culture."

The Loss of Social Capital and the Erosion of Trust in Public Institutions

Social capital is the value derived from social networks, institutions, trust, and reciprocity in a community or society.[33] It requires collective participation and moral imagination, in that social capital is only as positive or as strong as the people who invest in it. The need for economic security alongside social protections has never been greater, as changes in technology, coupled with higher levels of income disparity, poverty, and unemployment, and high volatility in the prices of food and other commodities, make companies increasingly interested in more "flexible" workers.

Building the capabilities to adapt to change requires a mix of embedded network ties, or bonding social capital, and arm's length ties, or linking social capital, rather than exclusive use of either. A mix of both provides access to the private resources in relationships and public information about markets. When social capital is eroded in networks and institutions, it denies people from different backgrounds the means to reconcile tensions between trust and cooperation as well as the control over resources and the achievement of cost efficiencies. By mobilizing different "types" of social capital, people in networks can create shared perceptions of value and shared expectations of success, but without this level of shared understanding, the tools for solving social problems are left to existing power structures.

One cause of the massive erosion of social capital comes from a scarcity mindset where people perceive a zero-sum conflict with economic and political issues. As demonstrated with decades of social science research by Robert Putnam, the decline of social capital, especially in key social and public institutions in the US that have served as beacons of civic engagement, has resulted in the partial or total disappearance of emotional and mental health support in communities, leading to increased social fragmentation

33. Coleman, *Social Capital.*

and a weakening of the ties that bind politically diverse groups, reducing their ability to be resilient.[34]

Conclusion: Blessed Are Those Whose Hearts Are Not Divided

C. S. Lewis offers an idea central to Sabbath economics in his 1960 book *The Four Loves*. He asks, What influences what we love and how we love, and how can we reorder our loves to put the loves that give the most glory to God back on top? We often imagine or expect an intentional spiritual practice, like Sabbath, as something that removes us from the world, but it did for Jesus the very opposite; he modeled what being in the world with God looked like. When we really examine what we love and how we love, Lewis's questions are an immediately useful place to start a Sabbath practice: What does it look like to be fully human, and how might I love better?

Sabbath is an immediate invitation to presence and connection in our everyday but our attention is our most valuable asset and yet we neglect to manage it. The late pastor and author Tim Keller powerfully argues in *Counterfeit Gods* that God wants our hearts, but the human heart is an "idol-factory," taking good things and making them into idols that drive our behavior.[35] Anything can be an idol, and it may not be the most obvious things—sex, power, money, status—that satisfy our needs. Keller argues that in a society where markets have failed to deliver on the American dream, many feel lost, alone, disenchanted, and resentful. Idolatry, quoting the nineteenth century philosopher Alexis de Tocqueville—who upon observing American society saw the disenchantment with life in times of austerity and prosperity—"comes from taking some 'incomplete joy of this world' and building your entire life on it."[36] Indeed, myths of the meritorious individual who

---

34. Putnam, *Bowling Alone*.

35. Keller, *Counterfeit Gods*, x.

36. Tocqueville, *Democracy in America*, 296, quoted in Keller, *Counterfeit Gods*, xii.

achieves it all alone, or financial wealth as the main route to satisfy the seemingly unquenchable pursuit of happiness, become idols in our hearts (Ezek 14:3). God warns people throughout Scripture that misplaced desire for gratification, control, and security will turn good things, like family, kids, or even a commitment to moral goodness into idols by expecting them to fulfill us and satisfy the longings of the heart.

Anglican priest and author Tish Harrison Warren points to an expanded view of renewing relationship, where Sabbath is not just a day, Saturday or Sunday, or the time we intentionally set aside to rest but can also be infused into actions big and small, in how we show up in moments that matter and in how we use our speech. Her main point, which underscores the critiques presented in this chapter of mainstream economic thinking, is that Sabbath as rest or ceasing first requires the fundamental act of letting go of control, of recognizing and accepting that we are a part of things we cannot understand, dominate, or measure.[37]

In practicing Sabbath this way, we surrender the false narratives of who social media and the marketplace say we are, what we can feel, what we can do collectively, and transcend these idols to see ourselves as belonging to Jesus. We become easily trapped in stories that do not serve us—binary, zero-sum, win-lose myths—instead of trusting our instincts that tell us we belong.

It takes an awareness of self and faith that God is in control to release the stories of scarcity that have been dominating our mindsets and keeping us alienated from one another and from the natural world. When we begin to be encouraged and intentionally participate and recreate a new collective story of belonging and kindness, of awe and sacredness, it is a reminder that death brings new forms of life—that rebirth and reemergence is the hope, the continuation.

What does it mean, then, to "reclaim" Sabbath from seeing it as just one day to engaging with it as *a prism* through which to construct our portfolio of economic relationships? We needn't wait until we reach our final days to learn that the "share of something"

37. Warren, "Can Everyone Take a Sabbatical?"

that is the most beautiful and meaningful, that brings us closest to God, are the memories that transcend our own life's timeline and transcend anything that we ourselves "did" or "knew" as a result of our actions. That we are able to observe the living world, see in a new way while we are alive, with every breath, and fully appreciate without needing to understand it, that is what Sabbath is about.

In so doing, we experience the wonder and awe around us in small and big ways, embracing the mystery of the Great Economy, which includes our death and resurrection into the kingdom of God as part of this larger story. We can practice Sabbath every day by welcoming the unknown, *training ourselves in waiting, hoping, and believing*. We often give in to easy resolutions, allowing authority figures or institutions to give us the certainty or the permission to remove our anxieties. But real freedom is not found in the addiction to certainty but in accepting what we don't know and cannot control and opening to wonder. Thomas Keating once said, "Silence is God's language and everything else is a poor translation." In the Bible's wisdom teaching, as explained by theologian Cynthia Bourgeault, "the proper translation of the Beatitude is, really, 'Blessed are those whose heart is not divided . . . whose heart is a unified whole.'"[38] Practicing Sabbath as the renewal of relationships means allowing our hearts to be fully present and love what is hidden in plain sight. It is a reminder that we can begin at any moment a contemplative practice of purification of the heart through the reordering of our loves.

Bibliography

Attenborough, David. Foreword to *The Economics of Biodiversity: The Dasgupta Review* by Partha Dasgupta. London: HM Treasury, 2021. https://assets. publishing.service.gov.uk/media/602e92b2e90e07660f807b47/The_ Economics_of_Biodiversity_The_Dasgupta_Review_Full_Report.pdf.

Berry, Wendell. *Home Economics*. New York: North Point, 1987.

Bourgeault, Cynthia. "Be Whole-Hearted." Center for Action and Contemplation, Apr. 20, 2017. https://cac.org/daily-meditations/be-whole-hearted-2017–04–20/.

38. Bourgeault, "Be Whole-Hearted," para 1.

Clark, Andrew, and Treanor, Jill. "Greenspan—I Was Wrong About the Economy. Sort of." *Guardian*, Oct. 23, 2008. https://www.theguardian.com/business/2008/oct/24/economics-creditcrunch-federal-reserve-greenspan.

Coleman, James Samuel. *Social Capital in the Creation of Human Capital.* University of Illinois at Urbana-Champaign's Academy for Entrepreneurial Leadership Historical Research Reference in Entrepreneurship. 1988. https://ssrn.com/abstract=1505872.

Crouch, Andy. *The Life We're Looking For: Reclaiming Relationship in a Technological World.* New York: Penguin, 2022.

Dasgupta, Partha. *The Economics of Biodiversity: The Dasgupta Review.* London: HM Treasury, 2021. https://assets.publishing.service.gov.uk/media/602e92b2e90e07660f807b47/The_Economics_of_Biodiversity_The_Dasgupta_Review_Full_Report.pdf.

Graham, Carol. *The Power of Hope: How the Science of Well-Being Can Save Us from Despair.* Princeton: Princeton University Press, 2023.

Hayhoe, Katherine. "The Biggest Uncertainty is Us." *New York Times*, June 26, 2022. https://www.nytimes.com/2022/06/24/climate/climate-forward-katharine-hayhoe.html?unlocked_article_code=1.sU4.l5Pi.H8MBZcwdUo7t&smid=url-share.

International Labor Organization. "Americans Work Longest Hours Among Industrialized Countries [. . .]." Sept. 6, 1999. https://www.ilo.org/resource/news/americans-work-longest-hours-among-industrialized-countries-japanese-second.

Keller, Timothy. *Counterfeit Gods.* New York: Dutton, 2009.

Minard, Sara "Higher Risk, Higher Principles: A Simple Investment Thesis for Christian Impact Investors." *Impact Alpha*, Nov. 17, 2021. https://impactalpha.com/higher-risk-higher-principles-a-simple-investment-thesis-for-christian-impact-investors/.

Myers, Ched. *The Biblical View of Sabbath Economics.* Tell the Word. Washington, DC: Church of the Savior, 2001.

Offer, Avner. "Between the Gift and the Market: The Economy of Regard." *Economic History Society* 50.3 (1997) 450–76.

———. "Economic Welfare Measurements and Human Well-Being." In *The Challenge of Affluence: Self-Control and Well-Being in the United States and Britain Since 1950* by Avner Offer, 15–38. Oxford: Oxford University Press, 2006.

———. "The Economy of Obligation: Incomplete Contracts and the Cost of the Welfare State." Discussion Papers in Economic and Social History Working Papers 103, Department of Economics, Oxford University, Oxford, UK, Aug. 2012.

Plumer, Brad. "Climate Change Is Speeding Toward Catastrophe: The Next Decade Is Crucial, U.N. Panel Says." *New York Times*, Mar. 20, 2023. https://www.nytimes.com/2023/03/20/climate/global-warming-ipcc-earth.html.

Putnam, Robert D. *Bowling Alone: The Collapse and Revival of American Community.* New York: Simon & Schuster, 2001.

Rohr, Richard. *Things Hidden: Scripture as Spirituality.* Cincinnati: Franciscan Media, 2008.

Ruskin, John. *"Unto This Last": Four Essays on the First Principles of Political Economy.* 2nd ed. Kent, UK: George Allen, 1877.

Saez, Emmanuel, and Gabriel Zucman. "The Rise of Income and Wealth Inequality in America: Evidence from Distributional Macroeconomic Accounts." *Journal of Economic Perspectives* 34.4 (2020) 3–26. https://www.aeaweb.org/articles?id=10.1257/jep.34.4.3.

Sandel, Michael. "Toppling the Myth of Meritocracy." *Harvard Gazette*, Jan. 5, 2021. https://news.harvard.edu/gazette/story/2021/01/the-myth-of-meritocracy-according-to-michael-sandel/.

———. *The Tyranny of Merit: What's Become of the Common Good?* New York: Farrar, Straus & Giroux, 2020.

Schweitzer, Albert. Selection from *Out of My Life and Thought: An Autobiography.* Translated by Antje Bultmann Lemke. New York: Henry Holt, 1949.

Smith, Adam. *The Theory of Moral Sentiments.* First published 1789 by Thomas Cadell (London). Oxford: Bennett, 2008.

Spear, Jeffrey L., and Lynn Stuart Parramore. "What Is Real Wealth? A Ruskinian Framework for Economic Justice." Paper presented at INET Conference, Paris, France, March 27, 2015. https://www.ineteconomics.org/uploads/papers/What_is_Real_Wealth_A_Ruskinian_Framework_for_Economic_Justice_Spear_Parramore.pdf.

Sull, Donald, et al. "Toxic Culture Is Driving the Great Resignation." *MIT Sloan Management Review*, Jan. 11, 2022. https://sloanreview.mit.edu/article/toxic-culture-is-driving-the-great-resignation/.

Thurman, Howard. *Jesus and the Disinherited.* Boston: Beacon, 1976.

Tocqueville, Alexis de. *Democracy in America.* Translated by George Lawrence. New York: Harper, 1988.

US Surgeon General. "New Surgeon General Advisory Raises Alarm About the Devastating Impact of the Epidemic of Loneliness and Isolation in the United States." US Health and Human Services, May 3, 2023. https://www.hhs.gov/about/news/2023/05/03/new-surgeon-general-advisory-raises-alarm-about-devastating-impact-epidemic-loneliness-isolation-united-states.html.

Warren, Tish Harrison. "Can Everyone Take a Sabbatical?" *New York Times*, June 25, 2023.

Wilson-Hartgrove, Jonathan. *God's Economy: Redefining the Health and Wealth Gospel.* Grand Rapids: Zondervan, 2009.

Chapter Nine

Sabbath as Redemption

Introduction

PHILOSOPHICAL AND THEOLOGICAL REFLECTION on the meaning of human work and leisure has been infrequent in the history of the West. While some scholars insist that the problems of work and leisure form a distinctly contemporary set of questions,[1] in my recent exploration of work I have demonstrated that they are an important part of the Platonic tradition of philosophy, which extends from the dawn of Western thought to the present day.[2] By

---

1. Most important among them is probably Simone Weil (1909–43), who maintained that "the Greeks knew about art and sport, but not about work." See Weil, "Mysticism of Work," 178–79. In her final book-length composition she reiterated this claim: "Our age has its own particular mission, or vocation—the creation of a civilization founded upon the spiritual nature of work. The thoughts relating to a presentment of this vocation . . . are the only original thoughts of our time, the only ones we haven't borrowed from the Greeks." Weil, *Need for Roots*, 92.

2. My own effort in this direction resulted in the publication of *Philosophies of Work in the Platonic Tradition: A History of Labor and Human Flourishing*.

focusing on the tradition established by Plato and continued by his many intellectual descendants over the centuries through the medieval and modern ages, I have tried to show that work has in this heritage been closely tied to contemplation, as much a matter of inner spiritual transformation as manipulation of the external environment, and conceptually linked to questions of justice and community life. Even more ancient is the problem of rest, one that arises in the Hebrew Bible and is given unique sanction in the Ten Commandments, which mention no other holiday. The Sabbath is certainly the first time in the ancient world that a day of rest was enshrined in religious and cultural practice,[3] and it is arguably the oldest holiday that the world still continues to celebrate, perhaps even the most important on the Jewish calendar.[4] Given the biblical injunction to "rest" upon the Sabbath, rabbinical tradition expended strenuous effort to determine what exactly "work" is. Only by knowing what counts as "work" can one *refrain* from working. Therefore a rich tradition of reflection on the meaning of "work" dates back to the Talmud, which posited a textual parallelism between Exod 20:10 ("But the seventh day is the sabbath of the Lord thy God: in it thou shalt not do any work")[5] and Exod 35:2

Because of this book's limitation in scope, I was not able to treat significant contributions to the philosophy of work offered by Aristotle and important modern thinkers of work like John Locke and Karl Marx. For similar reasons I largely avoided the question of leisure as such. This chapter is meant to address my omission of Hannah Arendt (1906–75), another key figure in the history of philosophy of work who is certainly more influenced by Aristotle than Plato and by the topic of leisure or rest. I am grateful for the opportunity to contribute to this volume, and I offer this chapter as a kind of supplement to *Philosophies of Work in the Platonic Tradition.*

3. See Blevins, "Observing Sabbath," 479: "Although there is debate about when and how weekly sabbath observance began to be practiced on a regular basis, this division of time into seven days with the seventh day designated as a day of rest for all was unprecedented in the ancient world. Peter Craigie has pointed out that 'there is no clear evidence of a *sabbath day* (or of time construed as a week) apart from the Israelite tradition.' John Tullock has called the practice of Sabbath observance 'one of Israel's most influential contributions to Western civilization.'"

4. See Epstein, *Jewish Holidays,* 12. See also Millgram, *Sabbath,* 1.

5. Scripture quotations throughout this chapter are taken from the KJV.

("Six days shall work be done, but on the seventh day there shall be to you an holy day, a sabbath of rest to the Lord"). Given that there followed immediately after the latter reference the instructions for building the tabernacle, all the tasks that followed were deemed "work" and therefore to be avoided on the Sabbath, beginning with the explicit injunction in the subsequent verse that "Ye shall kindle no fire throughout your habitations upon the sabbath day." Thirty-nine major categories of work were deduced, including sowing, reaping, threshing, and carrying objects from one place to another.[6] Thus was "work" described in detail in Jewish tradition so that it could be scrupulously avoided on the Sabbath. The more positive injunctions pertaining to ritual practice for what was to be celebrated (and how) derive their modern format from Rabbi Joseph Karo's (1488–1575) compendium of legal codes *The Set Table*.[7] In Christian tradition, however, due to neglect of the Sabbath, and due to a paucity of philosophical resources for thinking about work and rest, we have much less to draw upon than our elder brothers and fewer resources to inform our thinking on these subjects.

In this chapter I am turning to Hannah Arendt to complement my philosophical and theological exploration of the meaning of work and rest. Drawing on her philosophy, which springs mainly from the Aristotelian rather than Platonic tradition, and which has proven influential in discussions of work, I aim to complete her schema of activity (which she divides between labor, work, and action) with corresponding accounts of *in*activity (which I am calling play, leisure, and rest). Given her this-worldly perspective, she stands in some ways outside the Platonic heritage and the Christian theological tradition, so she will make a unique contribution to the problem at hand, one from which a theologically informed or Christian philosophy of work can still benefit. A German-born philosopher who made her career in the United States, Arendt is celebrated for her insights into totalitarianism, "the banality of evil" that she diagnosed at the heart of Nazism as

6. Millgram, *Sabbath*, 172–73.
7. Millgram, *Sabbath*, 174.

an eyewitness to the trial of Adolph Eichmann in Jerusalem, and the nature of the practical and theoretical lives, which she viewed through a lens grounded in deep appreciation of classical Greek and Roman sources. The bulk of Arendt's discussion of work appears in her seminal text *The Human Condition*, which is devoted to the question of the active life in human culture and history and thus by her own admission excludes the indisputably important role of theory and contemplation.[8] Part of her reasoning for this decision is that the notion of the active life, which has for the most part taken a proverbial back seat to the contemplative life in Western history, has thereby lost some of its nuance and internal structure. The simplest way to appreciate Arendt's key distinction is to locate it within this structure, which Arendt argues is tripartite. The active life is for her composed of labor, work, and action, each of which exhibits distinct characteristics.

I will first expound upon these three categories of activity, while anticipating my next section, in which I develop a further account of the three forms of inactivity in order to capture the active human life in its entirety. A complete human life will be spent in labor and play, work and leisure, action and rest. Furthermore, we will discover that labor relates to play, work to leisure, and action to rest in complex ways; I will argue that for Arendt each of the forms of activity "redeems" the prior form in a "vertical" dialectical interplay. For her, work redeems labor, and action redeems work, since each form addresses some intrinsic shortcoming in the prior. Going beyond Arendt, I will further argue that each of the corresponding forms of inactivity "redeems" the form of activity in an equally complex "horizontal" dialectical interplay. On my reading, play redeems labor, leisure redeems work, and rest redeems action. In every case, there is no strict opposition between the forms of activity and inactivity, but rather each shares features in common with their analogous pairing, while mirroring in reverse some of those same features.

---

8. See Arendt, *Human Condition*, 14–17. The theoretical life is the subject of her equally important book *The Life of the Mind*.

The third and final section of this chapter will exposit the redemptive power of rest, which stands in some continuity with Arendt herself but also departs from her in taking up an explicitly theological standpoint on the potential for human rest, which culminates for the religious thinker in worship as a specific type of rest. Inasmuch as Arendt herself does not expressly address the topic of rest as a correlate to action, I will try to remain in continuity with her thought, while when it comes to worship, which is a phenomenon that does not figure into her this-worldly account, I will admittedly be going beyond her own intention in order to grasp the full redemptive power of rest, realized in worship. Even so, I take it that theologians can benefit from her keen insights while recognizing that we may yet wish to build further upon them. In keeping with the spirit of this book, I intend to show that sabbatical rest is not merely a religious phenomenon (that it has wider implications for even the nonreligious) but that its fullest development can only be expressed in a transcendent direction.

Arendt on Labor, Work, and Action

These three species of activity are all connected to the fundamental conditions of human life. Labor ensures the biological survival of both the individual human being and humanity as a whole, and work furnishes the permanence that comes from the production of artifacts that to at least some extent perdure over time.[9] Both are anchored in our natality, inasmuch as they maintain and develop the world as a place of welcome to the newborn, who arrives as a stranger into a condition that is shaped by their predecessors and their laboring and working efforts. The titular human condition then is Arendt's primary interest, and it encompasses not just the biological facts of our coming into existence but anything into which human life has come in contact.[10] For purposes of clarity about how her distinctions are meant to function, we will briefly

9. Arendt, *Human Condition*, 8.
10. Arendt, *Human Condition*, 9.

look at some differences between work and labor, and then we will focus most especially on action, which is essential to what is to follow.

First, "labor is the activity which corresponds to the biological process of the human body, whose spontaneous growth, metabolism, and eventual decay are bound to the vital necessities produced and fed into the life process by labor. The human condition of labor is life itself."[11] For Arendt, labor is only to do with life and with meeting the necessities of life. This shows up in a variety of ways that she richly describes, but it must be kept constantly in mind that for Arendt these qualities of labor are just that: qualities of labor and not of work, which is different. By contrast, "Work is the activity which corresponds to the unnaturalness of human existence, which is not imbedded in, and whose mortality is not compensated by, the species' ever-recurring life cycle. Work provides an 'artificial' world of things, distinctly different from all natural surroundings. Within its borders each individual life is housed, while this world itself is meant to outlast and transcend them all. The human condition of work is worldliness."[12]

The relative stability and permanence of the process of work implies a different vector or directionality so to speak than that of labor. Labor is cyclical, while work is linear. The process of labor arises from nature and returns to it. On the most basic level, food is cultivated from the earth, it nourishes bodies, those bodies die, and they nourish the earth. These things Arendt says are the least artificial and most natural; they are features of human life that we have in common with other animals: "After a brief stay in the world, they return into the natural process which yielded them either through absorption into the life process of the human animal or though decay." The life of the living organism that participates in the cycle of labor and its products is also cyclical, arising from nature and returning to it in a sort of microcosmic imitation of the whole sweep of nature herself, which neither begins nor ends.[13] At

11. Arendt, *Human Condition*, 7.
12. Arendt, *Human Condition*, 7.
13. Arendt, *Human Condition*, 7.

the same time, the life of a human being also pursues a linear path, from birth to death, a course that presupposes a world that is in fact "not in constant movement, but whose durability and relative permanence makes appearance and disappearance possible, which existed before any one individual appeared into it and will survive his eventual departure."[14]

A final distinctive: Work is "entirely determined by the categories of means and end." A fabricated thing is an end product in two senses. First, it is the end in that a work process comes to a terminus in the product, and second, it is the end in that a work process is just a means for achieving the product. Labor too is a means-end procedure, but because labor doesn't reify or issue in a definite objective product, then it doesn't come to end when some definite result is attained; it comes to an end when labor power is exhausted. The worker stops when she has finished her work; the laborer stops when she is too tired to go on. As Arendt puts it, when it comes to work the end is never in doubt. Once "an entirely new thing with enough durability to remain in the world as an independent entity" has been produced, then the work is over. Labor processes though never end because they need to continue and be repeated to momentarily achieve an "end" that is more hiatus than terminus—a point forever just out of complete reach. It suffices then to distinguish labor and work on just this basis: Work has a definite beginning and a definite end.[15] Labor has no beginning and no end.

These observations will allow us to appreciate more deeply Arendt's third and final category, action. Action is for her the collective arena of speech and coordinated behavior, wherein decisions are undertaken and implemented. Action thus has a definite beginning (like work) but an indefinite, unpredictable end. Action too is irreversible, since putting a politically consequential course in motion cannot be contained once unleashed. Human beings can never predict or control the consequences of their collective action, and this is one feature that makes it different from labor

14. Arendt, *Human Condition*, 97.
15. Arendt, *Human Condition*, 97.

(which is, if anything, all too predictable in its endless cycle of needs and their satisfactions) and from work (which sets out from a definite plan and attains a predictable end at its completion). If the temporal structure of labor can be visualized as a circle, and that of work as a line with a beginning point and an ending point, then the temporal structure of action can be pictured as an arrow, with a beginning point but no end, aiming toward an unstable and uncertain future and thus combining features of both.

Three Forms of Inactivity: Play, Leisure, and Rest

The reason this is important is that each category of Arendt's analysis—labor, work, and action—can be thought of as having an analogue in the realm of *in*activity. This suggestion comes by way of Stephen Palmquist, who argued in a recent article that Arendt's clarifying and influential schema needs to be completed by three analogous categories, each of which bears some feature in common with its partner area of activity but also inverts each area of activity, like an obverse or a mirror that reflects the original in inverse form. According to Palmquist, "Balancing Arendt's three essential features of activity with three corresponding features of inactivity will give rise to a robust philosophy of work that exhibits specifically Christian implications."[16]

I now go on to introduce this completed schema of three activities and corresponding inactivities in order to show how the third category of inactivity, which Palmquist calls "rest," can be given richer content by comparison and contrast to Arendt's discussion of action. Following my exposition of how action opens onto an uncertain future, I will then argue that "rest," understood in a sabbatical sense and thus intimately tied to both community

16. See Palmquist, "Christian Philosophy of Work," 398. It should be noted that this proposal indeed extends Arendt's work in two ways: First, it adds to her schema three correlate species of inactivity; second, Arendt's account is avowedly this-worldly. As we will see, she takes into account theological doctrines like forgiveness of sin, but even then she abstains from developing the content of revelation as such and making a place for it in her book.

and worship, opens onto eternity. In accord with Palmquist's proposal, I intend to point the way toward a specifically Christian theory of work and leisure, while conceding with him that Arendt herself does not write from a Christian perspective. Jewish and Christian theologians will want to argue that the Sabbath as a religious holiday and given all that it implies was established by God and revealed in such a way that the "natural man" would not have devised on his own power or insight.

That being said, we will be considering how rest has a more general implication, of which one specific theological form might be sabbatical rest, which is in turn closely tied to worship. All cultures have had some practice of festivity or religiously significant abstinence or release from the bondage of political hierarchies and the urgency of economic transactions, so all cultures have had some recognition of the possibility of rest. All that we have to say about rest will be therefore arguably compatible with Arendt's view, though she does not speak at length about rest. Insofar as we are speculating about the specifically religious practice of sabbatical worship, however, we are going beyond the letter of Arendt's text. To name just one instance already remarked upon, for her, action opens onto an unpredictable future. For Jewish thinkers the Sabbath anticipates a future with some greater, though still unpredictable, content: the Messianic age. Similarly for Christians, worshipful rest anticipates an eschatological culmination in the parousia. Rest then would be open to a future that is not under human control in much the same way that action for Arendt is not fully under human control, but theologians are likely to want to give more texture and specificity to the eternal eventualities—also not under human control—foreshadowed by worship.

First, again in parallel to our procedure in the preceding section, we will, for the sake of clarity and to inform our discussion of rest, briefly linger over the two categories of inactivity that correspond to labor and work—namely, play and leisure.[17]

---

17. First, however, while I accept and hereby take up Palmquist's challenge to flesh out Arendt's scheme, I disagree with his correlations. Palmquist relates leisure to labor and play to work. I think it's the other way around. Arendt

I submit that play bears both similarities and contrasts to labor. Labor is imposed upon us by necessity; we labor to meet our needs. Play is entirely unnecessary but for the conventional rules that bind play. We submit when playing not to our needs but to the rules of the game. Play then is superfluous in one sense; we engage in it just for the sake of playing. In another sense though it is like labor in that when at play it is necessary that we submit to the logic of the game itself in order to play at all.[18] Similarly, just as the "products" of labor are expended as soon as they are produced in an endless cycle, so to play ends when it ends and leaves

---

herself maintained that the tendency of modern culture was only able to envision labor (all jobs being reduced in their meaning to something like "making a living" and having no other point or purpose), such that any activity dissimilar to labor gets coded as "play" (124). This disagreement may be terminological. I am thinking of leisure in the classical sense—namely, of retreat from burdensome practical and political obligations for the sake of not relaxation or idleness but cultivation of the mind in its free deployment. In ancient Rome *otium* was prized as the opposite of *negotium*. The latter is commonly translated as "business"; note that this is not the primary notion to the Latin-speaking mind but rather otium is, while negotium is formed grammatically by the simple affixing of the negative particle "nec." Business is thus not primary, and leisure, its opposite; leisure is primary, and business is what happens when one is not at leisure. The Roman patrician who retreats to his country manor does not do so to give himself over to idleness but rather to humane letters: reading and study. The cultural fruitfulness of leisure was given a classic exposition by Josef Pieper in his *Leisure: The Basis of Culture*. It is his sense of leisure that I have in mind. I again refer readers to my *Philosophies of Work in the Platonic Tradition* for a brief account of how the opportunity for leisure (once reserved for the wealthy in Greece and Rome) was democratized and enjoined upon all Christians by Augustine and Petrarch, among others. See chs. 3 and 5, respectively.

18. One might think of Bernard Suits's famous definition of a game: "To play a game is to engage in activity directed toward bringing about a specific state of affairs, using only means permitted by specific rules, where the means permitted by the rules are more limited in scope than they would be in the absence of the rules, and where the sole reason for accepting such limitation is to make possible such activity." Suits, "What Is a Game?," 148. According to this definition it is necessary to submit to a rule that is arbitrary. For example, the goal of the game is to get the ball in the hoop, but the hoop is ten feet off the ground. There is no *need* for the hoop to be ten feet off the ground apart from the fact that some kind of difficulty has to be interposed in order to make the game a game at all. That we all know I am talking about basketball is itself proof of how apposite and convincing this definition is.

nothing behind. Naturally a record of results—statistics of points scored, minutes played, etc.—can be made, but the game itself is *over*. Furthermore, play can always be taken up again in an endless cycle; it can always be picked up once more and just goes on and on for as long as it does and no more. It produces nothing but itself and for its own sake. Again therefore play exhibits a kind of gratuitousness that defies the necessity of hard labor but resembles its never-ending dynamism.

Leisure understood in the classical sense[19] is also inversely related to work. Work produces enduring objects that render the world familiar and stable. Leisure is not the absence of work but effort taken up in freedom and with the aim of producing not material artifacts but those of spirit and culture. Leisure according to Pieper's classic analysis is an attitude of mind that seeks not to bring anything about but rather contents itself with reality. Like God's approval of the goodness of his own creation, leisure is not work but appreciation of work and dwelling upon its goodness.[20] Work is a demonstration of mastery; leisure is a celebration of what is and what has been accomplished. Leisure thus issues almost indirectly not in artifacts of material production but in those of the heart and mind: arts, letters, theoretical insights. The products of work are eminently useful; leisure is decidedly nonutilitarian. It is the spirit that animates the liberal arts, those studies that "produce" landmarks of the human spirit. Like tables and chairs produced by work, these artifacts are lasting.

Palmquist is right to acknowledge that the ways of activity and inactivity are interrelated.[21] A complete human life will feature labor and play, work and leisure, action and rest. No life can be lived in one of these registers at the exclusion of the others any more than we can live an entire life awake and never sleeping. Moreover, we should think of these pairs as in some ways interpenetrating

---

19. See fn. 17 above.

20. Pieper, *Leisure*, 43.

21. Palmquist, "Christian Philosophy of Work," 399. He is right too that the medieval Christian tradition saw this as well. See Hanson, *Philosophies of Work*, chs. 3–5.

each other. While distinct, they are not ultimately separable.[22] As we have seen, labor and play bear something in common, and at its best, labor might take on some features of play.[23] Arendt too remarks upon this possibility, when she writes that "the blessing of labor is that effort and gratification follow each other as closely as producing and consuming the means of subsistence, so that happiness is a concomitant of the process itself, just as pleasure is a concomitant of the functioning of a healthy body."[24] The naturalness of labor is at once the imposition of necessity as well as the reward of gratifying our needs; like play, labor has its own intrinsic reward, the feeling of one's own vitality. Similarly, work is at its best when it is done in a leisurely manner, informed by a deep understanding of and appreciation for reality, the hand being guided by the head. Indeed, some of the most trenchant criticisms of contemporary work offered by the likes of John Ruskin and Simone Weil are that routinized, industrialized work precisely divorces contemplative guidance from practical production.[25] The best sort of work is informed by nonutilitarian insight brought to bear on the solution of a practical problem, one that does not override the reality of the world or of the human condition but is lovingly responsive to these realities.

This brings us to the final component of our study: rest. Rest, construed along sabbatical lines, is the obverse of Arendt's category of action. What is important here to realize is that just as play redeems labor and leisure redeems work, so too rest redeems

22. Again Palmquist is correct here. See "Christian Philosophy of Work," 406–7.

23. Think of the justly celebrated passage from Tolstoy's *Anna Karenina* that describes Lev's at first awkward but then immersive and absorbing attempts to mow hay with the peasants. His labor, the more he is able to align his body and soul with its natural rhythms, becomes gratuitous. Tolstoy, *Anna Karenina*, 316–327. Arendt herself says something similar about labor. "Labor but not work requires for best results a rhythmically ordered performance and, in so far as many laborers gang together, needs a rhythmic co-ordination of all individual movements." Arendt, *Human Condition*, 145.

24. Arendt, *Human Condition*, 107–8. The argument that pleasure is concomitant upon excellence is Aristotle's. See book X of the *Nicomachean Ethics*.

25. See Hanson, *Philosophies of Work*, chs. 7 and 8, respectively.

action. Furthermore, the higher levels of human activity redeem the lower. What this means is that each area of activity has its own endemic flaw. Labor never escapes the continuous pressure of bodily need: no sooner have we eaten then we are hungry again. Work can help redeem labor from this intrinsic affliction. Work, however, has its own endemic flaw. Work is as we have seen strictly instrumental, a matter of means that lead to ends. Work then is only a matter of what is useful and cannot answer the question of what in human life really *matters* or what we *should* as a human community be doing or making. As long as we are confined to thinking about efficient means for achieving given ends, any means will seem justified.[26] Action redeems work by placing it in a horizon of discussion about value and political decision making, which means work can be debated as to its quality and importance. Arendt explains this complex point as follows, using a significant choice of words:

> We have seen that the animal laborans could be redeemed from its predicament of imprisonment in the ever-recurring cycle of the life process, of being forever subject to the necessity of labor and consumption, only through the mobilization of another human capacity, the capacity for making, fabricating, and producing of *homo faber*, who as a toolmaker not only eases the pain and trouble of laboring but also erects a world of durability. The redemption of life, which is sustained by labor, is worldliness, which is sustained by fabrication. We saw furthermore that *homo faber* could be redeemed from his predicament of meaninglessness, the "devaluation of all values," and the impossibility of finding valid standards in a world determined by the category of means and ends, only through the interrelated faculties of action and speech, which produce meaningful stories as naturally as fabrication produces use objects.[27]

The crucial point here is that each sphere of human activity redeems the prior one from a constitutive limit or affliction.

26. Arendt, *Human Condition*, 229.

27. Arendt, *Human Condition*, 236.

Labor only answers to material needs; a life of nothing but labor would supply only what is required to keep on living. Labor on its own furnishes nothing to live *for*. The laboring life alone would be more animal than distinctively human. Labor knows only the never-ending cycle of natural need and its satisfaction, but work provides a world of stability, durability, and familiarity. Work "redeems" labor in that it produces the means of making labor more efficient (tools and technologies) and makes durable goods that answer to more than merely animal necessities. Labor can put food on the table, but work makes the table and the chair and the house, humanizing the worker's environment, making safe and comfortable surroundings, elevating what would otherwise be a merely bestial activity.

Work itself though is plagued by instrumentalism because it is lacking a larger horizon of value to dignify its products. Human beings can and do make chairs and tables and houses, but work cannot answer the question of why they should do so or go on doing so or what it means to sit around a table with family and friends. Action "redeems" work by giving it a context that endows the products of work with value and import. Through action we can assign a common and shared meaning, a sense of mundane ceremony, to the home, a shared life with family and neighbors, customs that dignify and interpret daily activities, modes of initiating the newborn into a world. Action redeems work by showing how we eat a meal together, why we say a blessing over our food, why we eat with chopsticks rather than fork and knife or why we use either rather than our fingers or why we use these fingers and not those. Action creates a horizon of meaning, shared stories that endow a human world with significance and an interpretive framework of values. In each case, the solution to the inner dilemma of one sphere of action comes from *outside* that sphere.[28]

Following Palmquist, though, we must have a complete picture of both inactivity and activity, and we must strive for a situation in which something of play colors our labor, something of leisure informs our work, and rest gives meaning to our action.

---

28. Arendt, *Human Condition*, 236.

In that case, not only is it so that the more advanced spheres of activity redeem the prior ones, the forms of inactivity also redeem the spheres of activity. We have seen that the burden of labor is lightened by the free spirit of play and that work is best done when informed by leisurely appreciation for reality and our own accomplishments in adding to, adorning, and putting permanence to our reality. In a similar way, rest will mark the limit to the political, showing that not all human communal undertakings are undertaken in pursuit of a political agenda. Corporate inactivity is restful; we engage in rest together to celebrate our community as one that is not exhausted by political or market relationships: we belong together in festivity and its concomitant relief from market pressures and political structures. Once again, this will be true in a general sense for all human communities, while for religious thinkers these forms of rest will be decidedly more worshipful and thus directed toward more specifically, if dimly, envisioned realities: the kingdom of heaven consummated on earth, the everlasting banquet, the new Jerusalem.

Rest as Redemptive

All that remains to be seen is how rest can redeem action, and with it the whole scope of human affairs. I will continue to use the word "rest," asking the reader to keep in mind that rest, conceptually and historically, is indissolubly tied to worship and festivity generally[29] and to community and especially domesticity.[30] In what

29. Pieper's classic text ends with a meditation on festivity, by which he means specifically religious celebration, keeping in mind that all cultural festivity, with its break with prevailing norms and exceptional status vis-à-vis mundane expectations and responsibilities, has its roots in religion. See *Leisure*, ch. 5. For him, leisure itself only finds its "fundamental justification" in religion, which makes of Pieper another ally in the case I am making here. Some effort has been made in our own day to rehabilitate the concept of festivity with the help of Korean-German philosopher Byung-Chul Han and Pieper. See Šokčević and Žvić, "Byung-Chul Han and Pieper on Festivity."

30. That the Sabbath should be celebrated in solitude or away from home is practically unthinkable in Jewish tradition. See Millgram, *Sabbath*, 8–14.

follows, I am both remaining faithful to Arendt's observations about rest and going beyond them. As a resolutely this-worldly thinker, she is insistent that rest "redeems" action from *within action itself*; a Christian thinker will however necessarily part ways with her on this score: the Sabbath as a religious observance is revealed by God, and worship is instituted in order to transcend the limits of this-worldly reality. For this reason, everything I have to say here about worship will go beyond the letter of Arendt's text. Furthermore, since she does not explicitly address the topic of rest, my reflections on this topic are (I hope) compatible with what she has to say about action, but they do constructively build on her foundation rather than faithfully exegete her own writing in *The Human Condition*. Using her thoughts on action then, I contribute my own thinking, inspired by Palmquist's suggestive expansion of her categories into corresponding areas of *in*activity for each of her three areas of activity. We have seen how work redeems labor and action redeems work. Now all that remains is to creatively complete this tripartite schema, thereby engaging Arendt, expanding on Palmquist, and offering a reading that is useful to Christian thinkers grappling with sabbatical possibilities. The Christian thinker will see the redemption of action through rest and worship as coming from *outside* the realm of action itself; Arendt is insistent that action is redeemed from *within* by forgiveness (which we will address further below; on this topic we can benefit from Arendt's insights on the nature of forgiveness while disagreeing with her about its divine power and provenance). Just as with labor and play, work and leisure, so too we find that action and rest bear some similarities but some differences as well; they are inverted, not opposites, and just as play is linked to but lightens labor and leisure limits and informs work so too rest will imitate in some ways and reverse in some ways action.

For Arendt, action arises from the plurality of the human condition. It presumes that people are equal, and thus able to in principle understand one another's speech and action, and that they are distinctive, or else there would be no need for people to make themselves understood by one another.[31] It is not the case that we just *are* distinct in scenes of action, rather we *distinguish ourselves* in speech and action; we present ourselves to one another as we are. In fact we cannot live in any other way. No individual *must* labor, and many people can spend their lives making use of the world and its artifacts without contributing to that world through work, but all persons must undertake words and deeds, without which a human being would literally have no place among others.[32]

Interestingly, worship, for Christian theologians, the crowning expression of "rest," is also, like action, necessarily communal and corporate.[33] To be "corporate" is to be embodied, and in worship the body of Christ assembles as a body and feasts upon the sacramental body and blood of Christ. In fact it is the body of Christ that makes the assembled congregation and indeed the whole church Christ's body in a second sense. Without this gathering of the body no worship is possible, which is why in the Anglican tradition at least Holy Communion cannot be celebrated by the priest alone; traditionally it can only be celebrated with at least one other participant. Again, like action, worship or rest is comprised of words and deeds. Speech employed in worship is rite, and liturgical ceremony is action. Worship has these two irreducible dimensions.[34] In speech we account for what we are doing, by the proclamation of God's word and the exposition of its meaning in a sermon, and in the recitation of prayers whose words have been shaped by generations of agreed-upon use as the best formulae for specifying with precision the contents of our hearts and minds. We also undertake actions that receive their meaning from our speech forms, breaking bread and pouring wine, laying hands upon the

31. Arendt, *Human Condition*, 175.

32. Arendt, *Human Condition*, 176.

33. In all descriptions of worship I am speaking from my own tradition of highly liturgical Anglicanism. All worship is to some extent "liturgical," but my reflections are informed by an elevated liturgical conception of ceremony (action) and rite (speech).

34. Arendt herself argues that speech and action are mutually disclosive; they cannot be separated. See *Human Condition*, 179.

elements, and distributing them to the people in a ceremonial order. We process in and out of the sanctuary, kneel for confession, stand to praise, sit to listen, and genuflect to reverence the presence of Christ in his body and blood when he is made present at the altar. These actions and words confirm us in who we are and allow us to be distinguished as who we are in Christ amongst other members of the body.

For Arendt, action is the scene of initiative, of newness. To act is to begin again, and as we have seen, all action initiates a vector that has a beginning but no foreseeable end. She writes, "With the creation of man, the principle of beginning came into the world itself, which, of course, is only another way of saying that the principle of freedom was created when man was created but not before."[35] This observation too dovetails with the biblical witness to Sabbath reality.[36] Karl Barth observed that the very first thing that human beings do at their creation is to participate in God's celebration of rest in appreciation of his creative work and its goodness. In the words of Angela Carpenter, "Barth's exegesis of the text in Genesis suggests that the command of the Holy Day is based on the fact that human time begins not with working or with the observation of divine working but with rest, celebration, and freedom. Humanity is created on day six, and therefore the first thing that human beings do is participate in the divine celebration of rest and joy in the goodness of creation."[37] She goes on to argue that "socially, the implications of this temporal ordering are profound. It means that rest, not work, sets the initial context for human activity, and it is to rest, not work, that this activity is repeatedly oriented."[38] According to the Christian tradition we are

35. Arendt, *Human Condition*, 177.

36. It is significant that here Arendt quotes St. Augustine, that great doctor of the church. "'That there be a beginning, man was created before whom there was nobody,' said Augustine in his political philosophy. This beginning is not the same as the beginning of the world; it is not the beginning of something but of somebody, who is a beginner himself." Arendt, *Human Condition*, 177.

37. See Carpenter, "Promise of the Sabbath," 85–86.

38. Carpenter, "Promise of the Sabbath," 86. Carpenter continues: "As Barth puts it, 'the first word said to him, the first obligation brought to his

therefore created *for* rest and worship, which redeem work and labor.

For Arendt, the newness or initiative always characteristic of action appears (in a choice of words that will prove significant) "like a second birth"[39] or in the "guise of a miracle."[40] In action the unexpected can be expected; the human being is able to perform what is infinitely improbable. How much truer is this of worship and rest? Is not the Sabbath the occasion of a weekly arrival of the unexpected? Does not worship herald the infinitely improbable, that salvation should be possible, that the redemption of the world has already been achieved and merely awaits its final consummation, week by week? For this second birth or miracle to be made the object of communal human experience, however, it must be, as Arendt puts it, "reified." "The specific content as well as the general meaning of action and speech may take various forms of reification in art works which glorify a deed or an accomplishment and, by transformation and condensation, show some extraordinary event in its full significance. However, the specific revelatory quality of action and speech, the implicit manifestation of the agent and speaker, is so indissolubly tied to the living flux of acting and speaking that it can be represented and 'reified' only through a kind of repetition."[41]

What interests us here of course is not art works but worship. The liturgy and rite too are reifications that glorify the mighty deeds of God and all that he has accomplished on our behalf. Because worship and rest are the *in*action of a community, however, a community that is dynamic and living, the meaning of these deeds must be stabilized, "reified," in an emulative practice, a kind

---

notice, is that without any works or merits he himself may rest with God and then go to his work.' For Barth, this means that Sabbath is the true time by which we understand all other time. We cannot think about and understand the working day without first understanding the Holy Day. It is the latter that provides the standard for human life and thus for grasping the true meaning of work" (86). Again notice how the Sabbath redeems work for Barth.

39. Arendt, *Human Condition*, 176.

40. Arendt, *Human Condition*, 178.

41. Arendt, *Human Condition*, 187.

of sacred drama that re-presents the deeds that are being memorialized and celebrated when we rest together. That it be repeated is essential to liturgy. The prayer of consecration in the Book of Common Prayer recalls that Jesus Christ "did institute, and in his holy Gospel command us to continue, a perpetual memory of that his precious death and sacrifice, until his coming again."[42] Thus does the liturgy itself reflect on its own necessarily repetitive structure. The drama of liturgy[43] is to be performed again and again until the return of Christ. It would not function as liturgy were it only undertaken once; its meaning is established by Christ at the Last Supper, but this founding moment is in a way a misnomer; there will be no last supper until the world itself comes to an end, nor could it be otherwise. Furthermore, this drama can have only a theoretical meaning apart from being spoken and reenacted. The meaning of the liturgy is not reducible to words on a page any more than the meaning of Bach's Violin Partita no. 2 can be reduced to notes on a page; they must be performed to be understood.

Continuing to consider this process of "reification" as a model for the deposit of the liturgy celebrated only in times of rest and not of action, we can with Arendt agree that human action consists in a kind of "web" (to use her metaphor) of relationships.[44] The imagery of a web suggests the intangible quality of human associations, which ramify outward from the subject of any one human speech act or deed in ties to multiple other humans with whom we all necessarily interact throughout our lives. While intangible, the web is nevertheless entirely real.[45] As naturally as fabrication produces use-objects, action produces "stories" that tacitly narrate the processes kicked off by the consequences of shared action. "Nobody," she tells us, "is the author or producer of his own life

42. Book of Common Prayer, 334.

43. The drama of liturgy is not a slavish aping of the instituting events; repetition is always repetition with difference. For more on this point in the thought of Søren Kierkegaard, see Hanson, "Naked Before God."

44. Arendt, Human Condition, 183.

45. Arendt, Human Condition, 183. On this same page Arendt expressly repudiates all forms of materialism in politics.

story. In other words, the stories, the results of action and speech, reveal an agent, but this agent is not an author or producer."[46] This is because nobody is wholly autonomous over their own lives but is rather caught up in the stories of their parents, siblings, fellow citizens, teachers, and so on.[47] "These stories may then be recorded in documents and monuments, they may be visible in use objects or art works, they may be told and retold and worked into all kinds of material."[48]

My argument is thus that we should think of the patterns of restful worship as reified repetitions of liturgical speech and action. Just as action is expressive of a person's place among their peers, and a "story" of a sort is mutually narrated by their shared relationships, a story that can be "reified" in artifacts that recount it, so too worship is a kind of reification of the Christian story. Participating in it reconfirms us in our identity before God, relinks us to our fellow believers in the church, and reminds us of our non-autonomy. While Arendt affirms that in action no one is the sovereign author of their own life, in worship the faithful have the opportunity to reflect on how much more so this is true for those who call God their Father, the one and only true sovereign. Just as our stories are not strictly ours to tell even when viewed from the lens of action, when we rest from action we rediscover that God is another author, perhaps the primary author, of our story. That coauthored story is reified and inhabited in the rest that redeems all other action.

Nowhere is this truth more conspicuous than in the drama of forgiveness, to which Arendt dedicates a chapter. It is striking perhaps that in a decidedly this-worldly account of human action Arendt chooses to focus on forgiveness. However, she presents forgiveness as a human phenomenon, a power within our grasp, and even interprets the teaching of Jesus of Nazareth as having

46. Arendt, *Human Condition*, 184.

47. Later in this same chapter Arendt directly refutes the pretense to sovereignty on the part of any human individual. "No man can be sovereign because not one man, but men, inhabit the earth." See *Human Condition*, 234.

48. Arendt, *Human Condition*, 184.

affirmed this very fact.[49] She is insistent that by turning to the doctrine of Jesus she is in no way claiming belief in the authority of Christ but rather recognizing only the political relevance of his teaching. "The discoverer of the role of forgiveness in the realm of human affairs was Jesus of Nazareth. The fact that he made this discovery in a religious context and articulated it in religious language is no reason to take it any less seriously in a strictly secular sense."[50]

Theologians may wish to assert the special prerogative of their own discipline to interpret the teachings of Jesus in a more than "strictly secular sense," but we should still appreciate Arendt's insights and apply them to our description of rest as a correlate to action. In fact, we might be led to disagree with her in one point. Recall above that she argued that work redeems labor from its continual submersion in the necessities of biological life, while action redeems work by endowing the products of human ingenuity with meaning. For Arendt, the possibility of redeeming action comes not from a higher sphere (for her there is no such thing) but from within action itself.[51] There are two problems she has in mind. First, action is open ended. Its final consequences cannot be envisioned from our present stance, but it does have consequences, which are woven into the webs of our lives and that cannot be reversed. Second, action is unpredictable. Its import is always running ahead of us, and consequences may follow from any action that are unintended or even regrettable. Forgiveness is the remedy for these endemic problems.

If I am right about rest being the redemptive correlate to action, then, just as all areas of human activity and inactivity find their final redemption for the Christian in worshipful rest, so too does forgiveness ultimately find its full expression only in rest.

49. Her choice of Scripture passages to support this contention is selective. This point has been effectively made by Paul Ricoeur in his *Memory, History, Forgetting*, 487. I have written on forgiveness in Kierkegaard's thought (for whom I argue it is a specifically religious phenomenon and not a natural one at all). See Hanson, *Kierkegaard and the Life of Faith*.

50. Arendt, *Human Condition*, 238.

51. Arendt, *Human Condition*, 236–37.

Apart from this point, however, much of what Arendt has to say is insightful and relevant to our account. How does forgiveness affect the quality of human action? Forgiveness she says undoes the deeds of the past, those consequences of action that were not intended nor desired. "Without being forgiven, released from the consequences of what we have done, our capacity to act would, as it were, be confined to one single deed from which we could never recover."[52]

This remarkable liberating capacity depends entirely upon the plurality of human persons that lies at the fundament of all action: no one can forgive herself (at least not without first being forgiven by another).[53] Forgiveness is the very opposite of revenge, which rivets its victim to her misdeed and almost automatically inflicts upon her the just deserts of it, locking both the victim and the perpetrator in an unbreakable cycle.[54] Forgiveness is the mini-miracle that breaks this cycle and ensures human freedom and the ongoing ability to begin something new, to initiate the unexpected. "Only through this constant mutual release from what they do can men remain free agents, only by constant willingness to change their minds and start again can they be trusted with so great a power as that to begin something new."[55] Despite her secular perspective, at this point Arendt admits that the love that disposes us to forgive smacks of "unworldliness." "Love, by its very nature," she concedes, "is unworldly, and it is for this reason rather than its rarity that it is not only apolitical but antipolitical, perhaps the most powerful of all antipolitical human forces."[56]

If then rest is the temple of love, if worship is where the love of God and love for fellow humans is felt most palpably and enjoined upon us as an ever-new commandment, then the church is not another political association at all but rather an antipolitical community. Here at last then we have identified a respect in

52. Arendt, *Human Condition*, 237.
53. Arendt, *Human Condition*, 237.
54. Arendt, *Human Condition*, 240–41.
55. Arendt, *Human Condition*, 240.
56. Arendt, *Human Condition*, 242.

which rest then is the obverse of action: rather than remain bound to the consequences of past action, in worship we are released to new freedom again, reminded of the newness of our situation. The corporate confession of sin and the proclamation of accomplished fact of those sins' forgiveness is thus a centerpiece of liturgical worship, for it constitutes the antipolitical nature of the community at worship. We might say therefore that Sabbath is the *time* of forgiveness; it is when the liberating power of forgiveness is unleashed. In the realm of action every deed has consequences. If forgiveness is able to "undo" those consequences, then rest is the "space" that makes that undoing possible. Rest implies the possibility of forgiveness and its redemptive power, because it means that no action is ever final and unrevisable after all; no word spoken is ever the last word.

It is perhaps not insignificant that Arendt ends her reflections on action with an appeal to the Gospels. Left to ourselves, she muses, all human affairs are in a sense doomed. We are all born to die, and it looks on the face of it as if mortality were the last word when it comes to the human condition. But this is not quite so even on her own grounds; in her words, action is "the one miracle-working faculty of man," another teaching she attributes to Jesus.[57] Action interferes with mortality and opposes itself to it under the auspices of natality. That we can be born is the ontological root of action, and this is "the miracle that saves the world." "It is, in order words, the birth of new men and the new beginning, the action they are capable of by virtue of being born. Only the full experience of this capacity can bestow upon human affairs faith and hope," two virtues entirely discounted by the pagan Greeks, for whom Arendt otherwise has so much appreciation.[58] By contrast, the triumph of faith and hope is hailed in the Christian tradition. "It is this faith in and hope for the world that found perhaps its most glorious and most succinct expression in the few words with which the Gospels announced their 'glad tidings': 'A child has been born to us.'"[59]

57. Arendt, *Human Condition*, 246.
58. Arendt, *Human Condition*, 247.
59. Arendt, *Human Condition*, 247.

So, for Arendt herself, to be clear and fair to her vision, the annunciation of the birth of Christ is ultimately a human phenomenon, the glad tidings are that we as human beings can be born, more possibilities for human action are always available, and forgiveness is possible for those actions that we repent of. A Christian theology of work and rest can profitably gain insight from these principles while still affirming that there is more at stake than just the birth of an ordinary child in the glad tidings of the Gospels. I have tried to show that we can accommodate much of what Arendt has offered us in a larger framework, one suggested by Palmquist as pairing forms of inactivity to the forms of activity Arendt so eloquently describes. If this larger framework is persuasive, we can see that just as, for her, action redeems work, which redeems labor, so too a redemptive power is operative "horizontally" as well as "vertically," so to speak, between the areas of activity and inactivity, as well as from one layer of activity to another. Play then would redeem labor, leisure would redeem work, and rest would redeem action. Rest, like action, is plural and corporate. For Christians, rest endows our lives with meaning, confirming us in our identities as children of God and fellow members of Christ's body. It performs the reality of our mutually interdependent stories, our lives being written in relationship with God and with one another. It is undertaken not only with a view to the uncertain future but indeed in anticipation of eternity. It enshrines the forgiveness of sins as a signal means by which action's consequences can be undone and we can be freed from the burden of past sin. Like action it valorizes birth and resists death. And while action proclaims the miracle of birth, rest proclaims the miracle of being born again.

Bibliography

Arendt, Hannah. *The Human Condition*. Chicago: University of Chicago Press, 1958.

Blevins, Kent. "Observing Sabbath." *Review and Expositor* 113.4 (2014) 478–87.

The Book of Common Prayer and Administration of the Sacraments and Other Rites and Ceremonies of the Church Together with the Psalter or Psalms of

David According to the Use of the Episcopal Church. New York: Oxford University Press, 2005.

Carpenter, Angela. "Exploitative Labor, Victimized Families, and the Promise of the Sabbath." *Journal of the Society of Christian Ethics* 38.1 (2018) 77–94.

Epstein, Morris. *All About Jewish Holidays and Customs*. Rev. ed. New York: Ktav, 1970.

Hanson, Jeffrey. *Kierkegaard and the Life of Faith: The Aesthetic, the Ethical, and the Religious in* Fear and Trembling. Bloomington: Indiana University Press, 2017.

——— "Naked Before God: Kierkegaard's Liturgical Self." *Kierkegaard Studies Yearbook* 24 (2019) 85–101.

——— *Philosophies of Work in the Platonic Tradition: A History of Labor and Human Flourishing*. London: Bloomsbury, 2022.

Millgram, Abraham E. *Sabbath: The Day of Delight*. Philadelphia: Jewish Publication Society of America, 1965.

Palmquist, Stephen. "Toward a Christian Philosophy of Work: A Theological and Religious Extension of Hannah Arendt's Conceptual Framework." *Philosophia Christi* 11.2 (2009) 397–417.

Pieper, Josef. *Leisure: The Basis of Culture*. Translated by Alexander Dru. New York: New American Library, 1963.

Ricoeur, Paul. *Memory, History, Forgetting*. Translated by Kathleen Blamey and David Pellauer. Chicago: University of Chicago Press, 2004.

Šokčević, Šimo, and Tihomir Žvić. "Byung-Chul Han and Josef Pieper on Festivity: An Attempt to Rehabilitate the Culture of Festivity in the Time of Mere Survival." *Bogoslovska Smotra* 91.5 (2021) 915–41.

Suits, Bernard. "What Is a Game?" *Philosophy of Science* 34.2 (1967) 148–56.

Tolstoy, Leo. *Anna Karenina*. Translated by Constance Garnett. Philadelphia: George W. Jacobs, 1919.

Weil, Simone. "The Mysticism of Work." In *Gravity and Grace*. Translated by Emma Crauford and Mario von der Ruhr, 178–81. London: Routledge, 2002.

——— *The Need for Roots*. Translated by Arthur Wills. London: Routledge, 2002.

Chapter Ten

A View from the Pew

James F. Longhurst and Kenneth J. Barnes

IN LIGHT OF THE insights above, the question of how one redeems Sabbath in practice remains. This is first and foremost a question for the church, and it may surprise some readers to learn that the church hasn't always agreed on Sabbath observance. As Gaffin rightly notes, there have been many differing approaches to the question, ranging from antinomianism (i.e., the obsolescence of the Decalogue in general), to strict Sabbatarianism (i.e., a rigid observance of the Sabbath ordinance's proscriptions).[1] Yet our thesis transcends even that debate. Our concern is not merely the observance of a religious ordinance but the reordering of life as a reflection of the created order. How may the church model the transcendent in ways that speak prophetically into the everyday lives of believers and nonbelievers alike? Below are vignettes that demonstrate both the need for Sabbath in everyday life and the benefits therein.

---

1. Gaffin, *Calvin and the Sabbath*, 11.

A Pastor's Journey Toward Resilience

Walking alongside the many people he has pastored over the past forty-two years has been a remarkable journey for Jim, a journey toward the lifelong practice of "Sabbath as resilience." His parish ministry began in rural Michigan, where he pastored a small, slow-paced farming community. Life there was not unlike the community in which he was raised, where the rhythms of life reflected the rhythms of nature. But even in rural Michigan, the stress and strains of modern life took their toll on him and his congregation. It didn't take long for him to realize that many small towns experience big-city problems, as people wrestle with the pressures of everyday life in an anxious and rapidly changing world. He soon found that the same could be said for people living in a highly sophisticated community of international thought leaders and practitioners in Geneva, Switzerland, where he led a church of Christian expatriates working at the cutting edges of science, technology, and finance. These gifted and successful individuals were at the heights of their fields, but the demands on their time, their talents, and their relationships could be crushing, even "soul destroying." There was little or no time for anything but work, and even less time for something as esoteric as Sabbath; and this was also the case for those he served in his final parish, the well-heeled, upwardly mobile denizens of suburban Boston. Every setting was unique, but the needs of the people were not.

Now in his seventies, Jim, a fellow pilgrim on the road to "Sabbath as resilience," holds before the people he serves the incredible opportunity to answer Jesus' invitation: "Come to me all you who are weary and heavy laden, and I will give you rest" (Matt 11:28). An invitation he once resisted himself.

Jim's story begins with a trip to the Holy Land in the late 1980s. The setting sun painted the sky pink as he and his companions bounced along in a bus winding its way up the hill to Jerusalem. The Jewish tour guide enthusiastically announced that they would arrive just in time for the start of *Shabbat*. The bus bumped to a stop, and its occupants found themselves at the famous Wailing Wall. While people streamed toward them from all directions, Jim's attention was drawn upward. "What was this?" he wondered, as he cast his eyes upon a group of young people who would change his perspective on Sabbath forever.

A large group of Jewish students had gathered at the top of a long, stone staircase. Singing all the while, the students lined up single file, each clasping the shoulders of the person in front of them. In this fashion, they snaked their way down the stairs and into an open space where they formed a large circle. Arms around one another, they danced and sang their welcome to *Shabbat*.

Jim never forgot the tangible sense of anticipation and delight in that Sabbath celebration. He described it as a rich experience—an amazing reality of people ceasing their work and transitioning into more than a mere respite from the mundane but into a celebration of both *shalom* (peace) and *chayim* (life). He tried to envision what it would be like to have something like that experience as part of his own work/life rhythms, but it was not to be, at least not for a while. Though he often shared the story with others, it didn't seem to translate into his own hectic life and pastoral ministry—that is, until he succumbed to a very common affliction among church pastors: the dreaded and debilitating effects of burnout.

Jim's experience is all too common, both inside and outside of the church. The pull to do more and achieve more is powerful. Nowhere is this more apparent than in American culture where "time is money" and what you do is the primary measure of who you are. Enter the need for Sabbath as an antidote to the destructive idols of insatiability and the "tyranny of now."

Even though Sabbath is deeply ingrained in the Judeo-Christian tradition, the practice of Sabbath-keeping is virtually absent among Western Christians, but that need not be the case. A unique opportunity exists for God's people to redeem Sabbath from its current state of religious relic to that of celebration—a Sabbath rest that gives meaning and purpose to everyday activities by seeing them through the prism of God's delight in creation.

As Lauren Winner notes,

There is something, in the Jewish Sabbath, that is absent from most Christian Sundays: a true cessation from the rhythms of work and world, a time wholly set apart, and perhaps above all, a sense that the point of Shabbat, the orientation of Shabbat, is toward God.[2]

Jim learned this lesson the hard way. It took suffering from burnout for him to realize just how much he needed Sabbath in his own life. He knew that he had to re-prioritize everything in his life, including his pastoral work, in order to establish a proper work/rest balance.

The first step in the process was for him and his family to practice a form of "Sabbath as resistance," by reclaiming significant amounts of time from their overloaded diaries for what came to be known as their "Mackinac revivals."

Jim and his young family would spend days at a time on Michigan's Mackinac Island, a small, tranquil island where there are no motorized vehicles, only horse drawn carriages, wagons, and bikes. Putting aside their devices and their work, they found themselves able to unplug from the distractions and the stresses that came to dominate their lives. Here they could renew their relationships with one another and with God; and for them, the island became a sacred place where they could reimagine the beauty of God's creation and glean from it the power of God's Sabbath. Jim had redeemed Sabbath for himself and his loved ones, and in doing so, found the energy and capacity necessary to pursue the next chapter of his life and ministry.

When called to their new church, Jim and his wife Jean had become so protective of their Sabbath-keeping, and so sure of its benefits, that they introduced the concept to their congregants in a way that changed many of their lives for the better.

Like many other Christians, some people in his new congregation had an awareness of Sabbath, and some had even practiced it on a regular basis, but none of them had appreciated the multifaced nature of Sabbath—a prism through which one may assess the everyday activities of life.

2. Winner, *Mudhouse Sabbath*, 19.

As Jim got to know the people, he heard story after story that pointed to their deep need for Sabbath rest. In response, Jim began working to build a culture of Sabbath-keeping. He enlisted the aid of church members and together they studied what the Bible and other Judeo-Christian writers had to say about Sabbath; and over several years they began to integrate elements of Sabbath into their everyday lives, inside and outside of the church.

Their church program was developed by and for themselves. It began in Sunday school with a study of Ruth Haley Barton's *Sacred Rhythms: Arranging Our Lives for Spiritual Transformation*. There were study groups and Sunday Sabbath "challenges" to build into each participant's week. Their worship services included moments of sharing how they may, or may not, have met those challenges and what they learned from them. Sabbath was no longer tertiary to their Christian walk; it was central to it.

Through it all, Jim maintained his own Sabbath practices, giving others a model of what a "redeemed" Sabbath might look like. Not only did this regular practice restore him personally, it allowed him to be fully present with those closest to him and with the people he interacted with each day. Jim took regular walks with his wife, renewing their commitments to God and each other, as they regularly took stock of their priorities. He spoke to the congregation, from the pulpit and in private conversations, about the restorative powers of the natural world when framed within the context of God's redemptive purposes. He prioritized prayer to help him keep Christ at the center of all he was doing; and was often seen taking prayer walks with others in the sanctuary as he prepared for his Sunday responsibilities. He had unconsciously woven Sabbath into the very fabric of his life and ministry.

Jim knew, however, that in order for the church to truly establish a culture of Sabbath-keeping, the principles and practices that he was modeling, would need to be incorporated into every aspect of church life, including the amount of work expected from church leaders and volunteers. He was careful to guard against the workaholic norms of the world creeping into the life and rhythms of the church. He soon discovered the importance of teaching regularly on Sabbath, so that it would become part of the church's DNA. His congregation benefited tremendously from this cyclical approach, annually revisiting the purpose of Sabbath and calling upon one another to stay faithful to the practice.

As discussed in previous chapters, experiencing Sabbath in all its fullness can be transformational in several areas: values, time, place, people, and faith. Jim witnessed this firsthand in the lives of his congregants. Below are some of their stories.

Sabbath as Reprioritization (Values)

> *If we do not allow for a rhythm of rest in our overly busy lives, illness becomes our Sabbath—our pneumonia, our cancer, our heart attack, our accidents create Sabbath for us.* —*Wayne Muller*

Laurie, an early-intervention specialist, worked with low-income families whose challenges and needs could be overwhelming.[3] She was also very involved in her church, often spending three or four evenings a week at meetings and Bible studies. Then her husband had a heart attack, and her world was turned upside down.

Donna, a retiree in her seventies, was as busy as ever. When asked if she might take time for Sabbath, she quipped, "I'll probably have to be laid up with a broken bone before I'll be able to slow down without feeling guilty about it." Little did she know that just months later she would find herself housebound, as the COVID-19 pandemic forced the world into "lockdown." For both Laurie and Donna, catastrophic and unforeseen circumstances, forced them to take stock of their values and led them to reconsider the healing benefits of Sabbath.

Looking back, Laurie sees her husband's heart attack as a wake-up call. She confessed that prior to his illness, they hadn't spent much quality time together. She noted that "if he had passed away at that point, I would have had regrets—even though all the

---

3. Names have been changed to protect anonymity.

things I was doing were good things." Her husband's "close call" forced them to reassess every aspect of their lives. Having reevaluated anything that might encroach on their time, their space, and their relationship, they soon became committed Sabbath-keepers.

In the quiet confinement of the pandemic, Donna experienced a slow but significant shift in her values. "I had taken a stab at Sabbath before, but reluctantly. This time was different," she shared. "I found myself asking, 'What *shall* I do today?' instead of 'What *should* I do?' I hadn't experienced that kind of freedom since I was a child." As the world reopened, Donna's new-found sense of Sabbath helped her guard against her propensity to overcommit. Sabbath is not a *part* of her week now, Sabbath is at the *center* of her week, and the decisions she makes about how to spend her time, where to go, and with whom to be are no longer driven by a need to keep "busy"; they are driven by her deepest and most cherished values.

Sabbath as Resistance (Time)

Nicole was a homeschooling mother of four. She was also active in her church, teaching Sunday School, leading children's programs, and planning events. Most weeks the items crossed off her to-do list were a small fraction of what she thought ought to be completed. As with many Americans, she often felt as though "there wasn't enough time in the day" to do everything that needed to be done. She was convinced that if she set aside time for Sabbath she'd fall so far behind that she'd never catch up. She was on a never-ending treadmill of seemingly endless activities, with barely enough time as it was to complete them. Or so it seemed.

"I must admit that I saw little value gained for so much time lost," Nicole remembers. "But I felt a gentle, yet persistent, nudge to give Sabbath a try. Metaphorically rolling my eyes, I tentatively dipped a toe into this seemingly pointless practice. I would love to report that after my first Sabbath I was hooked. I was not."

There were indeed missteps along the way, habits to unlearn, and practices that needed to be honed before Nicole began to experience the true value of a life lived within the rhythms of Sabbath; but eventually she discovered Sabbath's counterintuitive reality—that resistance to the "tyranny of now" doesn't waste time, it transforms it.

As discussed earlier, the first movement of Sabbath is ceasing—a tall order in the midst of the frantic pace that is often demanded of us. In her book *Mudhouse Sabbath: An Invitation to a Life of Spiritual Discipline*, Christian writer and speaker Lauren F. Winner recounts a story told by a journalist who was researching the Hasidic Jews in New York. This journalist asked her Hasidic hosts why God would care about ceasing work on Shabbat. Her host responded,

> What happens when we stop working and controlling nature? When we don't operate machines, or pick flowers, or pluck fish from the sea? When we cease interfering in the world, we are acknowledging that it is God's world.[4]

But ceasing to interfere in the world does not come easily, as Nicole quickly learned.

> That first Sabbath, I wandered aimlessly around my house, at a total loss. The dirty dishes called to me . . . yet I was obligated to ignore their cries to be cleaned. The laundry begged to be folded . . . but it had to stay piled in that basket where I could practically hear the wrinkles forming. It seemed I was foiled at every turn. By the end of the day, I had discovered a depressing reality: without a never-ending list of tasks to be done, I had no idea what to do with myself. Scarily, I wasn't certain I even knew who that "self" was if it wasn't immersed in gainful employment.

It was a rude awakening to be sure, but one that Nicole needed to experience.

Nicole, of course, is not alone in this realization. Many people struggle to separate their actions from their identity, and "ceasing"

4. Winner, *Mudhouse Sabbath*, 16.

is the first step toward that uncoupling. When we cease to measure our worth by the things we accomplish, we free ourselves to contemplate our value in God's economy, instead of the world's economy.

Sabbath as Reimagination (Places and Spaces)

Happiness, not in another place but this place[,] . . . not for another hour, but this hour. —Walt Whitman

Willow was a working mom who also cared for her live-in, disabled father. Even on her days off from work, she had to help her dad with everything from changing his clothes to providing his meals. She often wondered how she could practice Sabbath without abandoning her father in his time of need.

Ted worked remotely in a home-office located in his bedroom. Between Zoom meetings, interoffice communications, texts, and phone calls, he was reachable literally all day, every day. Unplugging for Sabbath was anxiety producing; what if he missed something important at work that needed a quick response? Could it cost him a promotion—or even his job?

As we have explored in previous chapters, Sabbath can transform even our ordinary places into spaces of sanctuary where we can find rest and renewal. Both Willow and Ted made this surprising discovery as they learned to practice Sabbath in the very spaces that demanded so much from them the other six days of the week. Willow's problem was one of constraint. She needed to be in a particular place at a particular time in order to serve her ailing father. So, she decided to "reclaim" the space she had by using it in sacred ways. In preparation for her Sabbath practices, Willow prepared everything for her father ahead of time, ensuring that even her kitchen was available for sacred use. Her home, while small, was sufficient for her simple acts of prayer and worship and for her time "alone" with God. Her home was no longer a place of mere utility, it was a place of worship, so that when Sabbath arrived, Willow was ready to receive its many blessings.

Ted's challenge was somewhat different. In his case, his sacred space had been invaded by his work and all the technical tools of his trade. Unfortunately, he didn't have many other options in terms of his home office. So, Ted decided on a two-track approach. First, he made the conscious decision not to check work communications during his Sabbath time, or to even enter his home office during that time. Then, he decided to create a new, sacred space in his home that was only to be used for Sabbath-related activities, such as prayer, meditation, Bible reading, and precious time with family and friends. What looked to some as little more than a renovated back porch with a screened-in gazebo, some comfortable furniture, and a cozy fire table was in fact holy ground where Ted was finally able to quietly reflect upon and reconnect with God and the people whom he loves most.

Sabbath as Renewal (People)

Matt taught sixth grade in a town where high-powered parents had great expectations for their children's education. They paid high property taxes, and they expected their local educators to produce "results." It was a very stressful environment for everyone, from the administration to the teachers and staff to the students themselves. Between grading schoolwork, planning the following week's curriculum, and writing reports, Matt's Sabbath could easily have been swallowed whole, and along with it, any opportunity for connection with God or with the people God had placed in Matt's life.

As a senior in high school, Faith's schedule was jam packed. She was taking a full course load, doing volunteer work, applying to colleges, and pursuing several extracurricular activities. She believed that her future depended on how well she could keep all those balls in the air, and she worried that if she devoted significant time to Sabbath, they would come crashing down, along with her hopes and dreams. At times, she was lonely and missed the fellowship that church life afforded her, but she had been groomed to believe that her primary focus in life had to be preparation for her future. Fellowship was a luxury she didn't think she could afford.

While Sabbath can include individual time with God, at its heart, it is a communal experience. God's people experience Sabbath more fully when they journey toward God together, as both Matt and Faith would soon learn.

Matt discovered that his Sabbath time encompassed more than rest when he spent it with others; it offered deep renewal. "When I think of the times that I have experienced true Sabbath," he reflected, "it's often been in the context of relationships with other brothers and sisters in Christ. Walking alongside others— seeking and finding God together—is much more powerful than going it alone." He had experienced firsthand the damage caused when one's work demands interfere with Sabbath-keeping. Relationships between believers become strained, and even our relationship with God becomes labored. Conversely, he found that when our Sabbath time is nonnegotiable, and our relationships with one another and with God are at the center of our Sabbath experience, wonderful things happen. Our rest produces renewal, and our worship animates our faith. His Sabbath-keeping didn't change the fact that he worked in a stressful environment, but it did give him the resilience and refreshment he needed to survive.

Similarly, Faith decided that despite the apparent "risks" associated with diverting herself away from the demands of her hectic life, she needed Sabbath more than ever. She especially needed the relationships that were at the heart of her Sabbath practices. She found that she loved spending time with people in a different season of life than her own. People such as her grandmother, her adult neighbors, and older friends from church offered Faith unique perspectives on the meaning of life, her values, and her preparations for the future. Through the lens of those relationships, she was better able to see the many ways in which God may be preparing her for a future of God's choosing and not society's choosing. Sabbath renewed her preparations for this life by keeping her grounded and focused on eternal life.

Sabbath as Redemption (Faith)

As discussed throughout this book, Sabbath-keeping begins with ceasing, much like the dimming of a theatre's lights precede the raising of the curtain. It sets the stage for respite, but it also sets the stage for redemption. Redemption happens when we immerse ourselves in an environment that allows us to connect with God, with creation, with others, and with our inner selves. This is how God fills us up and prepares us to get on with the mission for which we have been chosen. It is not an exhalation of the busyness of the week so much as it is an inhalation of all the good that God has in store for us. It is a steady and unrelenting process of continual reprioritization, resistance, reimagination, renewal, and redemption.

Shepherded by Jim, many members of his congregation experienced this progression from respite to redemption in their own lives, and of great importance was the intergenerational nature of their practice. Sadly, many of today's young people have no frame of reference from which to conceptualize Sabbath. Growing up in a society that idolizes being busy above almost all else, children have come to expect that feeling tired, harried, and stressed is just how life works. It has become so normalized that they don't even question it. They do, however, experience the toll this frantic way of life takes on them, and when it all becomes too much, they invariably deal with it in unhealthy ways. Often this looks like a collection of kids with necks at right angles to their bodies, their fast-flying thumbs the only indication that they are, indeed, conscious, as they stare zombie-like at their devices. Instead of dealing with life's "big-picture questions" (questions that ultimately have to do with faith), they escape the reality of their own existence and seek solace in virtual worlds.

When even this fails to distract, more sinister forms of coping emerge, such as alcohol and drug abuse, self-harm, and many more distractions and vices. Talk to any teacher or youth worker and you will get an immediate sense of how pervasive this is—and how dangerous. They speak of an increasing fragility in children, an inability to form meaningful relationships, and a lack of meaning and purpose in their lives.

The good news, however, is that children who do experience "redemptive" Sabbath can learn to trade-in their frenetic, high-tech lives for more balanced, holistic ones, but only if they are connected to more seasoned practitioners of Sabbath who can show them the way forward. This kind of intergenerational connection tends to be a lost art across most sectors of society today, but the church is one place where it still reigns supreme.

When people, young and old alike, engage in the Sabbath practices of rest, reprioritization, resistance, reimagination, renewal, and redemption, they are allowing themselves to know and be known by God and to know and be known by one another. This becomes a stream that flows through everything, each and every day, filling the faithful to overflowing, that God's light may illumine the darkness both in us and around us.

As has been suggested above, the most important part of leading a Christian congregation in Sabbath is not found in a program, or in a list of rules and procedures. It is much more than that; in order to be effective, it must be fundamental to the overall mission of the church.

To be missionally oriented is to recognize that the faithful serve a God who *sends* them into the world to bring redemption, and recovering the gift of Sabbath is one tool God has given us for the fulfillment of that mission.

As mentioned at the beginning of this chapter, Jesus himself once intoned to his bedraggled followers, "Come to me, all who are weary and burdened, and I will give you rest. Take my yoke upon you and learn from me, for I am gentle and humble in heart, and you will find rest for your souls" (Matt 11:28–29 NIV). Jesus invites us to rest so that we might know who God is and respond to God's invitation by continuing God's work.

The work of the kingdom, however, is not meant to be done alone, and as Christians we are all called to share God's peace and redemption by walking faithfully with Jesus, in a way that reflects his divine nature. The faithful would do well to remember that, when God created the world, God stepped back and looked upon his handiwork; not because he was tired and weary but because he delighted in his work and in his creation. But creation isn't merely an event; it is a process, and it is one that God invites us to be part of.

There are many ways for congregants to step back from their labors and rest in the goodness of God. It is, first and foremost, a choice that the pastor asks of the congregation, a choice to trust in God's sovereignty, to accept the invitation daily, to be a part of God's mission, and to rest in the rhythm of life that God has established from the beginning.

While time-away moments are essential, regular Sabbath-keeping gives congregations the opportunity to emulate the divine in every aspect of life. In times of worship and fellowship, on Sundays and throughout the week, and in groups, large and small. In the practice of Sabbath, the people of God stand in solidarity with Jesus as he rejects the Pharaoh-like commoditization of humanity, which enslaves us, in favor of an invitation to "seek first the Kingdom of God" (Matt 6:33 NIV), instead of the kingdom of Mammon. (Matt 6:24).

The Bible tells us that as the people of God prepared to enter the promised land, God's parting words to Joshua were, "Be strong and courageous, do not be frightened or dismayed, for the Lord your God is with you wherever you go" (Josh 1:9 NIV). The same words may apply today to any pastor who dares to promote a practice as countercultural and antithetical to modern sensibilities as Sabbath-keeping. It will strike many as irrelevant and impractical, legalistic and archaic. In fact, it is none of those things. It is a remarkably relevant and imminently practical antidote to the social ills wrought by postmodern capitalism and its many related tyrannies. Far from being proscriptive, it is a free gift from God; and while it may be an ancient practice, its power and its blessings are in great need and short supply, even today.

It was in the context of challenging the *status quo*, by healing the sick, supping with sinners, and feeding the hungry, that Jesus reminded his followers that Sabbath was made for humanity's sake, and not vice versa (Mark 2:1–28). And so, in the face of all that disturbs, distracts, disorients, and debilitates us, we would do well to remember that Sabbath is, after all, the ultimate form of resilience.

Bibliography

Gaffin, Richard. *Calvin and the Sabbath: The Controversy of Applying the Fourth Commandment.* Nairobi: Mentor, 2009.

Winner, Lauren F. *Mudhouse Sabbath: An Invitation to a Life of Spiritual Discipline.* Brewster, MA: Paraclete, 2003.

About the Authors

Kenneth J. Barnes

Kenneth J. Barnes is a fellow of the Royal Society of Arts, the Mockler-Phillips Professor of Workplace Theology and Business Ethics, and the director of the Mockler Center for Faith and Ethics in the Public Square at Gordon-Conwell Theological Seminary. Prior to his academic career, Barnes spent many years as a senior international executive doing business on six continents. His main areas of research and teaching are the intersections of faith, work, and economics. He has published numerous papers in the US, UK, and Australia; his recent book projects include *Redeeming Capitalism* (2018), "Religion and Business Ethics: Religious Perspectives on Business" in *Routledge Companion to Business Ethics* (2018), and "Faith, Work and Economics: A Mission of the Church, a Mission to the Church" in *Transforming Work* (2024). He is married to singer-songwriter Debby Barnes, is a father of three, and a grandfather of four.

C. Sara Lawrence Minard

C. Sara Minard is the associate director of the Mockler Center for Faith and Ethics in the Public Square at Gordon-Conwell Theological Seminary. She earned her PhD in economics (highest honors) from Sciences Po, Paris, under the tutelage of Nobel Laureate Amartya Sen, for research on social entrepreneurship in the informal economy in Senegal, where she served as a small business volunteer with the US Peace Corps (1998–2000). An academic, advisor, educator, and consultant, Minard is adjunct professor of international and public affairs and the Brandmeyer Fellow for Impact and Sustainable Investing at Columbia University's School of International and Public Affairs. She lives on a multi-generational family farm in northern New Jersey.

Autumn Alcott Ridenour

Autumn Alcott Ridenour is the Mockler Associate Professor of Christian Ethics at Gordon-Conwell Theological Seminary and a senior research fellow at the Mockler Center for Faith and Ethics in the Public Square. She is author of *Sabbath Rest as Vocation: Aging toward Death* (2018) and the forthcoming volume *Restlessness and Belonging: Augustinian Wisdom for the Digital Empire*. She also serves on the editorial board for the *Journal of the Society of Christian Ethics*. She enjoys time with her husband, Jay, and their three children, and fellowship with their church community in Sudbury, Massachusetts.

Larry O. Natt Gantt, II

Larry O. Natt Gantt, II, is Professor of Law and the inaugural Associate Dean for Academic Affairs at High Point University Kenneth F. Kahn School of Law and visiting fellow of the Mockler Center for Faith and Ethics in the Public Square. Professor Gantt previously served as Executive Director of the Program on Biblical Law and Christian Legal Studies and Lecturer on Law at Harvard Law School, and as Professor and Associate Dean for Academic Affairs at Regent University School of Law.

Professor Gantt's scholarship has focused on two primary areas: (1) law school academic support and legal education reform and (2) legal ethics and professional identity formation. He has also been actively involved in the well-being movement in legal education and the legal profession; and he currently serves on the American Bar Association Commission on Lawyer Assistance Programs's Advisory Commission and on the board of the Institute for Well-Being in Law as vice president of law schools.

Natt is an active member of Wesley Memorial Methodist Church in High Point, NC. He and his wife Meredith are blessed with four wonderful daughters.

Kara Martin

Kara Martin is a lecturer with Mary Andrews College (Sydney), an Adjunct Professor at Gordon-Conwell Theological Seminary, and a visiting fellow of the Mockler Center for Faith and Ethics in the Public Square. Kara serves on the Board of Theology of Work Project (U.S.A.). Previously, she served as Associate Dean of the Ridley College Marketplace Institute (Melbourne), and has worked in media and communications, human resources, business analysis and policy development, for a variety of organizations. A leading light in the Faith at Work movement, her highly acclaimed books include: *Workship: How to Use your Work to Worship God* (Graceworks, 2017), *Workship 2: How to Flourish at Work* (Graceworks, 2018), and *Keeping Faith: How Christian Organisations Can Stay True to the Way of Jesus* (w/ S. Judd and J. Swinton, Langham, 2024)

Kara is married to David, and together they run a home maintenance business. They worship at Harbourside Baptist Church and love kayaking, and being walked by their border collie Archie.

Jeffrey Hanson

Rev. Dr. Jeffrey Hanson, an ordained priest in the Anglo-Catholic tradition of the Episcopal Church, is Senior Philosopher for the Human Flourishing Program at Harvard University, Associate Professor of Philosophy at New College of Florida, and a senior research fellow of the Mockler Center for Faith and Ethics in the Public Square. Dr. Hanson's writings on Kierkegaard, French phenomenology of religion, and the arts are motivated by an ongoing interest in the practical value of philosophy for human flourishing. His publications include: *Kierkegaard as Phenomenologist: An Experiment* (ed., Northwestern University Press, 2010), *Michel Henry: The Affects of Thought* (ed. w/ M.R. Kelly, Bloomsbury, 2014), *Kierkegaard and the Life of Faith: The Aesthetic, the Ethical, and the*

Religious in "Fear and Trembling" (Indiana University Press, 2017), and *Philosophies of Work in the Platonic Tradition: A History of Labor and Human Flourishing* (Bloomsbury, 2023). He lives with his wife and teenage son in Sarasota, and he is serving as priest-in-charge of St. Luke's Episcopal Church in Fort Myers.

James F. Longhurst

Jim Longhurst is a senior fellow of the Mockler Center for Faith and Ethics in the Public Square and executive director of Clapham Servants, a global non-profit organization that seeks to serve humanity in and through the person and work of Jesus Christ. His main areas of interest are "conversations of consequence" in the public square, the intersection of faith and work, mentoring, discipleship, and congregational well-being. As senior pastor of an international congregation in Geneva, Switzerland, and pastor of churches large and small in the United States, he has seen firsthand, the transformative power of the gospel for individuals, organizations, and cultures. He is an avid swimmer and a fiercely competitive croquet player. He and his wife, Jean, love spending time with their two children and three grandchildren.

Peter S. Heslam

Peter Heslam is a fellow of the Royal Society of Arts, the director of Faith in Business, Cambridge (UK), and a visiting fellow of the Mockler Center for Faith and Ethics in the Public Square. He has research interests at the interface of business, faith, and development, as well as in the life and work of the public intellectual, social entrepreneur, and statesman Abraham Kuyper. Heslam's interdisciplinary scholarship reflects his academic background in social science, history, ethics, missiology, and theology. After serving on the faculty of the London Institute for Contemporary Christianity (LICC), he has held various appointments at the Universities of Oxford and Cambridge and as a visiting professor at various research institutions around the world. His recent publications include editing the Abraham Kuyper anthology *On Business and Economics* (2021).

www.ingramcontent.com/pod-product-compliance
Ingram Content Group UK Ltd.
Pitfield, Milton Keynes, MK11 3LW, UK
UKHW020223210425
457661UK00005B/227